JOHN'S MESSAGE

GOOD NEWS FOR THE NEW MILLENNIUM

VAL WEBB

Abingdon Press
Nashville

John's Message: Good News for the New Millennium

Manufactured in the United States of America.

05 06 07 08—10 9 8 7 6 5

TABLE OF CONTENTS

MEET THE WRITER

Dr. Val Webb is from Brisbane, Australia. She has lived for many years in Rochester, Minnesota, where her husband is a surgeon at the Mayo Clinic. They have three grown children and two grandchildren.

Dr. Webb has had numerous careers in her lifetime. She has a graduate degree in microbiology and pursued a research career at the University of Queensland, Australia. Later, in Rochester, Minnesota, she opened and owned Val Webb Galleries, an art gallery featuring art from all over the world, including her own. She also has published books on art.

When her family returned to Australia in the 1980's, Dr. Webb, while Superintendent of Communication and Resources for The Wesley Hospital, Brisbane, a Uniting Church hospital, began religious studies at the University of Queensland as part of her own spiritual journey. At the same time, she chaired the commission responsible for theological and lay education in the Queensland Synod of the Uniting Church of Australia (a union of Methodist, Presbyterian, and Congregational churches). Dr. Webb completed her Ph.D. in systematic theology at Luther Seminary, St. Paul, Minnesota. She also co-founded The Open Table in Rochester, a center for education around peace, justice, and global awareness.

Dr. Webb now divides her professional life between adjunct teaching at the University of Minnesota in Minneapolis and writing for thoughtful, seeking lay persons. Her book *In Defense of Doubt: An Invitation to Adventure* (Chalice Press, 1995) addressed some of these questions. Her latest book, *Why We're Equal: Introducing Feminist Theology* (Chalice Press, 1999), offers resources to persons in the church for understanding feminism as the very heart of the Christian church's call to a discipleship of equals. Her home church is Christ United Methodist Church in Rochester, Minnesota.

A WORD OF WELCOME

Welcome to JOHN'S MESSAGE: GOOD NEWS FOR THE NEW MILLENNIUM. We hope you enjoy this fresh new look at the Gospel of John. This six-session study will enrich your understanding of this Gospel and will provide a worthy pursuit of the gospel truth as we approach and live in the third millennium.

This study is thematic; it does not begin with the first chapter of John and proceed through reports of Jesus' ministry to the Resurrection. Rather, the study is organized around six life-oriented questions that will help you examine in a renewed way the life and teachings of Jesus.

The Six Questions

As the new millennium begins, many of us will have turned our minds to what the new century will bring and what it means for us. The sessions in this study help us with that reflection. Listed at the top of the next column are the questions around which the sessions in this study are organized:

What was John's world like?
What was John's Gospel about?
What does John teach us about the human condition?
What does John teach us about Jesus Christ?
How does John teach us to understand our times?
What does John teach us about living in the third millennium?

Within each lesson there are ample references to the Scriptures that illumine the responses to the question. When possible, we have tried to let John speak to us afresh today.

Studying John Successfully

JOHN'S MESSAGE can be used successfully as a self-study or as a group study. Reflection and discussion questions are in boxes at the bottom of the pages throughout the book. The questions refer to information on that page or on an adjacent page. The square ■, triangle ▲ ▼, circle ●, or diamond ◆ will direct you to the section of the page that prompted the question.

Use these questions for quiet reflection or as conversation starters. Some of them ask for data: When did something happen? What did Jesus say or do about an event or experience? Others ask for more evaluative responses: Why, do you think, did Jesus treat someone in a particular way? Still other questions personalize the Gospel: What does this ancient teaching mean for you or for the church today?

In each instance, the text will draw you closer into John's world and help you bridge the centuries from the time when Jesus lived and taught to your time, when Jesus' teaching remains alive and vibrant for today.

Reflection Partners

If you are studying John in a group or on your own, you may want a reflection or prayer partner to talk to and pray with during the time between the study sessions. There are more than enough discussion starters to sustain a class; you have more questions to pique your interest than you can cover. You may enjoy pursuing the questions on your own or praying with a partner about the concerns that arise during the study time.

Making a Commitment

You may find during or at the end of your study that you are ready to affirm or reaffirm a commitment of your life to Jesus Christ. We encourage you to reflect carefully on the message Jesus Christ brings to you through the words of John. Do these words engage you to grow into a deeper, more complete relationship with God? Do they bring new light to biblical passages that had been unclear or a stumbling block to real understanding?

If you are inspired to a new level of commitment, discuss it with your pastor, your study leader, or a committed friend in the faith. You will find support and welcome.

1

JOHN'S WORLD

Undated Letters and "Good News"

One thing that frustrated my father was undated letters. He would carefully file letters he received, but only after adding the full date and often a note about its circumstances or context—why it was written, by whom, and from where—if this were not clear in the letter. Because of this, I now have a collection of correspondence to my parents at different stages in my life and from different places.

My father's editorial changes from a hastily scribbled "Monday 6th" or "Wednesday 14th" to month, year, and location means that "Dad, this time I really will fail Chemistry" can be read as the panicky voice of a first-year college student. When a letter enthuses about our daughter's first step, his notes remind me which daughter and at what age she accomplished that feat. Without these editorial additions that anchor my past in time, much of the meaning behind my letters would be lost, distorted, or reduced in significance.

● The Gospels are like letters from the past. However, not only are they undated, they also talk of unfamiliar events, people, places, and customs. The Gospels also have come down to us through many layers of translation and editing. What makes it even more difficult for today's readers is that the Gospel writers, as I did in my letters to my parents, made assumptions about what their readers knew and so did not always include details needed to fully appreciate their stories today.

● Before you begin this study, share any feelings you have about how the Gospel of John has been important in your life. These may include problems it has raised, as well as comfort it has brought. Have you found it an easy book to read?

The Gospel writers also made selections (as I did writing to my parents) as to what information was important for the readers in their particular situation. The author of John's Gospel tells us twice at the end of the Gospel that only some of the many signs Jesus did in the presence of his followers have been recorded (John 20:30-31). He further said that, if they all were written down, "the world itself could not contain the books that would be written" (21:25)!

Early Days and Modern Time

I don't know about you, but these tantalizing words at the end of John's Gospel cause a shower of questions to pop up in me like water through holes in a garden hose. What other stories and sayings were not included? Why did the author think the included stories would best convince his particular readers? And who were these readers who needed convincing and reassuring anyway? Since "come to believe" (20:31) can also translate "continue to believe," what was happening in the readers' world that might be threatening their allegiance to Jesus?

■ Such questions make us aware that we twenty-first–century readers have some groundwork to do in recreating from this distance, as best we can, the circumstances or "world" of this Gospel, in order to faithfully "hear" what was good for these people in their circumstances. Only then can we decide, with the help of the Spirit, how and why this message might be good news for us in the third millennium. Our first task is to do what my father did: date and locate the Gospel, asking to whom it was addressed and why the author felt so compelled to write.

The title for this study, JOHN'S MESSAGE: GOOD NEWS FOR THE NEW MILLENNIUM, reminds us of something very important. We are not here to study an ancient piece of writing called "The Gospel of John," but to "listen in" on a message of good news conveyed to a specific group of people as comfort in the bad news of their situation. "Gospel" (the English translation of the Greek *euangelion*) means exactly that: "good news being proclaimed," just as prophets announced the good news of God's intentions for the Hebrew people (Isaiah 40:9; 41:27; 52:7). It was not until the middle of the second century A.D. that the term *gospel* shifted from its primary meaning of oral proclamations of God's good news to the written record of these proclamations.

With our modern reverence for the written word (a written contract is more binding than an oral agreement, and ideas gain more credibility when published), we often give more attention to the exact words of the Bible. We forget to listen for the word from God—the good news being communicated way back then, in different ways and for different audiences.

Difference and Distinctiveness

▲The Gospels were not limited to the four in the New Testament. Different followers of Jesus wrote others over the first few centuries that, for many reasons, did not make it into the New Testament canon of books. Many scholars exhibit renewed interest today in these Gospels and in other writings from Jewish and Christian history uncovered in the 1940's at Qumran (the Dead Sea Scrolls) and in the Nag Hammadi Library in Egypt. These writings help illuminate the culture and context behind the events recorded in the New Testament Gospels so we can better understand the struggles faced.

Most biblical scholars agree that the New Testament Gospels cannot simply be read as eyewitness accounts written by Jesus' disciples, with the differences and discrepancies between them mere variations of what the reporters saw. The differences are more significant than that.

Jesus was crucified before the Passover meal in John's Gospel and after in the other three Gospels. Mark and John omit the story of Jesus' birth, something that became central in Christianity. If we simply merge the four stories into a composite account, including details from one Gospel but not another, we mask important clues to be discovered from the differences.

▼ Instead, scholars believe these Gospels were written at different times and places, recording

■ How would you define "good news"?

▲ If you are in a study group, share what you know about any of the Gospels other than the four in the New Testament. Do you know why they were they not included?

▼ What do you find difficult about reading ancient stories set in times, places, and cultures you have little knowledge about? What is most helpful to you then, in your study of these stories?

▼ Read John 21:24-25. What difference does it make to you that the author of John's Gospel only included a fraction of the things Jesus did and said? Why do you feel this way?

and interpreting the faith stories of different communities that formed around different followers of Jesus—stories tested through trials and struggles within the maturing communities that needed to be remembered for successive generations. Such written records became particularly important toward the end of the first century as the eyewitnesses of Jesus died.

Many Faith Communities

● We know there were many faith communities or house churches scattered across Asia Minor in New Testament times, with different teachings according to the witnesses to Jesus who founded them. Paul tells us that the Galatian church was divided because unnamed teachers had come into this community preaching a "different gospel" (Galatians 1:6) urging Gentile converts be circumcised.

Paul's letter to the Corinthian church pleads for unity in the face of quarrels between groups claiming allegiance to different teachers and messages (1 Corinthians 1:10-12). In Ephesus, Paul encountered disciples who had become believers through John the Baptist and did not know that the Holy Spirit was given at baptism (Acts 19:1-5).

These different communities were still a part of Judaism until around A.D. 80–90, attending the synagogue as well as meeting as house churches. Thus they also differed, not just regionally across Palestine and the Roman Empire, but within themselves with their different ratios of Jews and Gentiles and different allegiances to their Jewish roots.

■ As twenty-first–century Christians, we have the advantage of these community stories assembled as the New Testament. Because of this, we often assume there was uniformity in the message being proclaimed. In the first few centuries, however, this was not so. With no New Testament to

● Look up these texts from Acts and the New Testament letters. Identify as many situations as you can where conflicting teachings were creating problems for different fledgling faith communities. What was the issue of disagreement in each case? What do they tell you about the early church communities? How are they like our own community of faith? How are they different?

■ What differences or conflicting stories or events have you noticed in your reading of the four Gospels? Is this important to you? Why or why not?

JOHN'S MESSAGE

consult as authoritative, isolated fledgling communities struggled, often with only their founder's teaching.

Occasionally, itinerant teachers brought new ideas to share, which sometimes conflicted with what the faith community had already heard. Any collection of the stories and sayings of Jesus being written down in some communities (which became the source material for later Gospels) could only be circulated by physically copying them and then physically delivering them.

Just Who Was Jesus?

▲ There were also no agreed-upon statements as to who Jesus was, and many diverse views were offered as we see from the writings of early church leaders responsible for deciding which were orthodox and which were heretical. Not until the fourth century did church councils agree on what teachings about Jesus would be formalized in the creeds we have today. The differences in the Gospels, therefore, tell us a lot about the particular communities to whom they were addressed—what they believed and what was happening in their midst to necessitate the particular message of good news.

As transmitters of good news, the Gospels did not claim to be definitive, historical biographies transmitting every known fact about Jesus without any personal comment. Rather, they were like extended sermons or reasoned arguments, explaining to their readers why they should believe and urging them to do so (Luke 1:4; John 20:31). A writer selected his stories and arranged his discussion according to what would be good news for his audience.

Making the Good News Known

▼ Paul's address to the Greek philosophers of Athens is a good example of this. He did not present Jesus as the fulfillment of Jewish prophecy and hopes as he did with Jewish audiences, but as the one through whom the unknown god of the Greeks, who had created all nations to inhabit the whole earth, had spoken to

▲ What is the difference for you, if any, between the written words of the Bible and the message the Bible is trying to proclaim? What do you think it means to say the Bible is the inspired word of God?

▼ What do you think is the difference between a biography about a person and a piece of writing aimed to persuade you to believe what that person teaches?

them. As a result, some philosophers, who had previously heard him addressing Jewish audiences and thought he babbled about a foreign religion, believed (Acts 17:16-31).

◆ The writer of John tells us this is what he has done in his Gospel. He explains that he was not interested in recording everything there was to know, but in selecting and organizing his material and comments so that, by the end of the Gospel, his readers would be convinced that their belief in Jesus was well-founded (20:31, and also 21:24).

As twenty-first–century readers, we have to "listen" to the Gospel on these grounds. First, we must listen for why the writer thinks believing in Jesus is important for these particular readers. He will remind them of situations Jesus faced similar to theirs, of predictions Jesus made now being fulfilled in their lifetime, and of promises from Jesus that assure them God is still accessible to them. All this will give us clues as to the audience's concerns and trials.

Second, we can expect to find information about the community's life prior to the Gospel, especially something about the original founders of this community on whose eyewitness testimony the community's beliefs are based.

Third, we will hear stories about Jesus, interpreted for this community of faith through the guidance of the Spirit in their midst (14:15-27).

Documents, Dates, and Debate

When faced with any ancient document, twenty-first–century minds first want to know where it was written, by whom, when, and why. With the Gospels, such questions create problems.

First, the Gospel writers did not have my father there to scribble the day, month, and year on the top of the papyrus sheet! Second,

◆ Can you think of other revered documents created, not by one writer offering his or her personal opinions, but as a statement of a group of people's beliefs and goals, honed through the struggles of their life together? Do you know the actual authors? If so, do you agree with the statement because of what it says, or because of what you know about the author or authors?

● Does knowing that what became a part of our Scripture had been circulated orally, changed, embellished, edited, and then written influence its authenticity for you? What test do you use to determine the weight and influence of a text for you?

we do not necessarily have the first edition of the document.

● The New Revised Standard Version of the Bible carefully brackets any passages that are not included in all available copies of an ancient text, reminding us that such writings were not considered final when they were being used by the early church. As they were copied and circulated in communities, new memories, other stories, and new ways of interpreting the stories came to light. These also became part of a community's written record. What we have in the New Testament is the form of the document finally included in the official canon of books in the fourth century A.D.

As for John's Gospel, we know from comments by different early church writers that such a manuscript was in circulation around A.D. 130. However, because John's Gospel is radically different from the other three Gospels, which were gaining importance in early Christianity, there was considerable debate over whether to include John in the emerging collection of sound writings. Its popularity among groups being declared heretics at the time did not help.

The content of John's Gospel was not the only issue. The reliability test for a gospel, given the variety in circulation, was whether its teachings could be traced back to an eyewitness follower of Jesus. At this time, the origin of the teaching was more important than the person who finally recorded it on behalf of the community.

The Gospel titles we have today—Matthew, Mark, Luke, John—were assigned toward the end of the second century to distinguish the writings and give some indication of the possible origins of their teachings. There was disagreement about John's Gospel. Even when Irenaeus, Bishop of Lyon, declared it orthodox at the end of the second century and supported the assignation of its teachings to John, son of Zebedee, the debate continued—and still does.

The Identity of John

■ What does the Gospel itself tell us about its origins? We are left in little doubt. The founder and source of this Johannine community's faith was the "disciple whom Jesus loved," the beloved

---

■ Research these Scriptures about the beloved disciple and the sons of Zebedee. If the beloved disciple is not John, the son of Zebedee, what does that mean to you? Does not knowing make a difference in how you read this Gospel? Why or why not?

disciple (19:25-27, 34-35; 20:1-10; 21:20-24). But who was he (or even she, as some have wondered, given the prominent place of women among the disciples in John's Gospel)? It is important to note from the start that, in John, the term *disciple* is never restricted to the Twelve but is a more inclusive term for the followers of Jesus (6:60-71; 1:35-51).

The beloved disciple could have been a follower other than one of the Twelve. This Gospel makes no connection between the beloved disciple and John, son of Zebedee, even when the sons of Zebedee (only mentioned twice in John's Gospel) and the beloved disciple are mentioned in the same story (21:2, 7). Nor does this Gospel include the stories in which the sons of Zebedee feature in other Gospels (Mark 1:19-20; 10:35-45; and so on).

We are therefore in the dark, beyond the fact that he was the one Jesus loved. It really doesn't matter. The important thing the Gospel tells us is that he witnessed the events of Jesus' life and death and testified their truth to the community that gathered around his teachings after Jesus' death.

The Origin of John's Gospel

We also do not know who finally shaped the teachings received from the beloved disciple into this Gospel. Keeping in mind that the Greek word for "has written them" also refers to the source of information, "the one who taught about the events," we know that whoever wrote the Gospel was recording the testimony of the beloved disciple that he and his community knew to be true (19:35; 21:24). The writer was also convinced that if all the things Jesus did were recorded, the whole world could not contain the volumes (21:25).

This hint that others could, and might, write the "other things Jesus did" speaks to the community's desire to preserve the witness of this disciple as best they could for future generations. Since this statement follows a discussion with Jesus about how and whether the beloved disciple would die, perhaps their venerated founder had recently died, forcing the community to preserve his teachings while they remembered them clearly.

The important thing is that, for this community, what is written is true because the teachings can be traced back to one who was with Jesus and was loved by Jesus. (Traditionally, there has been a link made between John's Gospel, the three letters of John, and Revelation. Rather than wonder if the author was the same, it is more helpful to think of whether they came from the same community or tradition of teaching at later stages in its history. Despite our lack of information as to who this beloved disciple might have been, I will, for clarity, still refer to John as the writer, to John's Gospel, and to the community as the Johannine community.)

Insiders and Outsiders

What do we know about this Johannine community at the stage this Gospel was written? Again, we have to look for clues in the text. Most scholars locate this Gospel in a community, perhaps in Ephesus, around A.D. 90–100. Like the second- and third-century church writers, they see John's Gospel as the latest of the four Gospels. There is no space in this study to develop all the arguments for this, but I will highlight a few that are relevant to our understanding of the Gospel message.

Unlike some other New Testament writings, John says very little about a future return of Jesus (*parousia*). In Paul's letters and in Mark's Gospel especially, this was expected during the disciples' lifetime or soon thereafter.

▲ By A.D. 70–80, when Jesus had still not returned, parousia hopes were either projected into the future, or, as we find in John, seen as a current reality in the community as the presence of the Spirit. Rather than talking of a coming reign of God, John speaks of the presence of God (*Paraclete*) in their midst. The Paraclete not only will interpret the meaning of Jesus never completely understood by the disciples during his lifetime, but also will guide the community in new circumstances that would come their way (15:26–16:15). This change of emphasis suggests a Gospel date close to the end of the century. It is in John's Gospel that we get the fullest development of the role of the Spirit sent to the believers in Jesus' place.

"The Jews"

▼ There is no doubt John's Gospel talks about "the Jews" differently from the other Gospels. Jesus was a Jew throughout his life. He did not separate from

---

▲ Use a Bible dictionary to do some research on the *Paraclete* (see also *Advocate*). Then read John 15:26–16:15. What is the role of the Advocate or Paraclete?

▼ From John's language about "the Jews" rejecting Jesus, can you see potential problems for later Christianity and its relationship to Jews? Do you think it was necessary for such a complete break to occur between Judaism and Christianity over their interpretation of Jesus? Why or why not?

Judaism but advocated its transformation through his message of the coming reign of God. Many of his followers, including Paul, were Jewish, interpreting Jesus' life and teachings within Judaism.

The Gospels of Matthew, Mark, and Luke can be seen as responses to a "family argument"— dissension in the household of Israel among the people of God as to who Jesus, one of the family, was. These Gospels assure their audiences, even when such belief begins to threaten their acceptance in the synagogue and Jewish traditions after the Jewish War of A.D. 70 (the situation in Matthew and Luke), that they have come to the right conclusions about Jesus.

In these three Gospels, Jewish opposition to Jesus is still described as from the Jewish authorities. The language however, has changed in John's Gospel. As we shall see, Jesus is no longer portrayed as a true fulfillment of Jewish hopes. Jesus is now portrayed as the replacement of Jewish institutions, the new location of God's revelation—the new Temple and place of worship, the replacement of the Passover Feast, the ritual symbols of water and light, and more. John is at pains to show his community that, in Jesus, rather than in the synagogue and Jewish rituals, God is now encountered. Those who believe this are the true family of God (8:34-36; 13:33-35; 14:18-21) as opposed to the Jewish claim. ◆

Believers and Unbelievers

As John tells story after story of folk encountering Jesus and choosing to believe or not believe this, the gap widens between believers as those who dwell in the light and are not of this world, and unbelievers who choose darkness and the world. The criterion for being children of God no longer depends on Jewish heritage, but on believing or not believing, whether Jew, Gentile, or pagan. We are left in no doubt, from the start of John's Gospel, on which side "the Jews" who reject Jesus fall (1:10-13).

Expulsion From the Synagogue

We get a clue as to what has happened between the time of the

---

◆ Read these passages about the "true family" of God. What do they tell you about how this family is identified? How large is the family of God for you? What are the boundaries?

other three Gospels and of John from the story of the healing of the blind man. Followers of Jesus were not put out of the synagogue until long after Jesus' death—Jesus himself worshiped and taught there throughout his life.

● Yet in John's story of the blind man, he adds an editorial note as to why the blind man's parents refuse to answer the questions of "the Jews." They were afraid they would be put out of the synagogue (9:20-22; see also 12:42-43). Furthermore, John reminds his readers that Jesus told the disciples the night before his death that, in the future, those who thought they were offering true worship to God (16:2) would put them out of the synagogue.

■ This threat had obviously become reality for the Johannine community, and the fear of the parents and John's reminder of Jesus' prediction would speak volumes to them. We know from history of a "Benediction Against Heretics," introduced into Jewish synagogue liturgy around A.D. 80–90, that prays that apostates, Nazarenes (Christians), and the Minim (heretics) be uprooted and blotted out of the Book of Life. All the other evidence for dating this Gospel after A.D. 90 supports this most compelling evidence that John was addressing a community torn from its Jewish roots and identity because of their belief in Jesus. John's Gospel was written to assure this expelled community now undergoing the trauma of redefining itself over against Judaism, that they, not "the Jews" still in the synagogue making that claim, are the true children of God.

● Read the story of the man born blind (John 9 and also 12:12-43). If you wish, assign roles to different group members who will retell/recreate the story, pressing their own point of view. What was at stake for the healed blind man? his parents? the Jewish leaders? the people who saw the healing? the disciples? Jesus? (You will take a closer look at the commentary on this story in Lesson 3.)

■ What do you think it was like in Jesus' day to believe Jesus was the Messiah while worshiping in a synagogue that did not agree with you? How would you have argued your case? Can you think of parallel situations in Christianity today?

■ From your knowledge of Jewish beliefs and the Old Testament, why do you think it was so traumatic for the Johannine community to no longer claim its religious roots through Judaism?

The True Family of God

▼ As we read John's Gospel then, we will discover the recurring theme of insiders and outsiders. Some people over the centuries have used John's Gospel to support their own particular arguments as to who are the true people of God, making John's message an exclusive rather than inclusive message of good news.

Throughout this study, we will ponder this from our twenty-first–century perspective. In a pluralistic world, we will examine what John might tell us about belonging to a cosmic family of God no longer resting on narrow associations with one religious tradition, but on categories of believing and not believing something, whoever we are.

◆ John's marginalized and excluded outsiders were assured that their belief that, in the man Jesus, the God from the beginning of the world and beyond was somehow encountered was not a misplaced idea. Rather, this belief made them children of this God, true insiders. This was the good news for them. How is this the good news for us?

▼ From your reading in John's Gospel prior to this study, were you conscious of any strong insider-outsider language? If so, how did it make you feel—comfortable or uncomfortable? Why?

◆ Do you feel like an insider—a child of God? How is this good news for you?

◆ Jesus said, "Those who love me will keep my word, and my Father will love them, and we will come to them and make our home with them" (14:23). Take time in prayer, if you wish, to answer the question for yourself that Jesus asked Peter, "Do you love me?" (21:15-19).

2

JOHN TELLS HIS STORY

Like a great opera, the most breath-taking of paintings, or Shakespeare at his finest, the Gospel of John takes us soaring to the skies and reaching into the very depths of our being as the story unfolds of God's unfaltering commitment to be in relationship with humanity. The dramatic contrasts between those who eternally abide in the most intimate of embraces and those who obstinately tread a tragic path deeper and deeper into the eternal night of darkness, spell out a cosmic drama far beyond human comprehension. ■

As readers, we are not just asked to examine some facts and come to some intellectual conclusion about God reaching out to the world, but are drawn, whether we like it or not, into an encounter with God that demands a crucial decision from us. As the symphony builds to the heights and recedes into whispers, repeating the central theme with hundreds of variations, the Gospel writer pulls out all the stops of literary and spiritual persuasion to urge us to see and believe. It is not surprising that Clement of Alexandria, a leader in the early church, concluded that John had composed a spiritual Gospel in comparison with the more earthly stories of Matthew, Mark, and Luke. ▲

Caution: God at Work

While all the Gospels have variations in their emphases and themes, Matthew, Mark, and Luke have historically been called the "Synoptic" Gospels, because they present similar (synoptic) perspec-

■ What appeals to you about John's language? Do you have a favorite among the pictures he paints (vine and branches, good shepherd, bread of life)? What does it say to you?

▲ What, from what you now know about the Gospel, draws you to see and believe?

tives on Jesus, which suggest they shared common traditions and sources about Jesus for writing their Gospels. ▼ John's Gospel is very different. Even though Jesus is the central character, this Gospel is primarily the story of God. We are told this right at the beginning. While the other Gospels start with the story of a man called Jesus, John begins with the "Word" (*Logos*), which dwells, not in the realm of human existence, but "with God." Not only was this Logos with God, but it was God (1:1).

Logos in the Jewish Community

I am going to use this Greek term *Logos* instead of the English translation "Word," not to confuse you, but because "Word" does not convey the full meaning of what John was saying by using this descriptive term for God's activity. It also avoids us reading back into John what we think "Word" means, rather than let John develop his unique image for us.

◆ What did John mean by using *Logos* to talk about God? We find a clue when John reminds his readers (1:18) that no one has seen God, a fact central to Jewish understanding. It was thought that, if you looked on the face of God, you would die (Exodus 33:18-23). If no one has seen God, how then does one talk about God?

In the Christian tradition, we casually use "God" as if it is a name identifying a particular person or entity—something we can point to and say, "That is God." In Judaism however, people were hesitant to use the revered name of God (YHWH) whom they had never seen. ● Instead, they used descriptive terms for what they encountered as the divine at work in their history: attributes such as

▼ Check a Bible dictionary, a Gospel parallels reference, or your study Bible to compare the texts of the Synoptic Gospels with John. Can you see some common themes in the Synoptic Gospels not found in John? Why do you think this is?

◆ What does John's Gospel have as its introduction instead of the birth story of Jesus? Read John 1:1-18. This sounds more parallel to Genesis 1 than to the birth narratives in Matthew and Luke. What does John's prologue tell you about God's creation?

● Look up these Old Testament attributes of God. Say in your own words what they tell you about God. What metaphor or metaphors, from Scripture or from your own experience best describe your experience of God?

glory (Exodus 33:18, 22; Habakkuk 3:3-4), goodness (Exodus 33:19), speech (Exodus 3:4), presence (Isaiah 43:5), refuge (Psalm 59:16), and sustenance (Psalm 42:1-2; 65:9-10) to name a few.

The Hebrew writers were not saying God was a river, a voice, or a warrior, but rather that this was how they experienced or "knew" the divine in their midst; "God at work" in their world. It did not bother them that they had not seen God. God's activity among them, creating, revealing, and protecting, was ample assurance God loved them and was committed especially to them as the chosen ones of God (Genesis 6:18; 9:8-10, 15; Exodus 3:7-8; 19:3-6).

■ Therefore, when John's readers heard the word *Logos* being used by John to talk about God, they would immediately assume that it was, as always, a descriptive term for God's activity. And *Logos* was not a new term for them. It was the Greek word that translated "the word of God" used so often in the Hebrew Scriptures. However, when God spoke in Hebrew history, it was not just words—a revelation—but also had creative power. God did something through speaking (Genesis 1:3, 6, 9, 11, and so on).

Like other descriptions of God's activity in lieu of actually seeing God, this description of God, the "word of God" creating and revealing through "speaking," took on an almost independent existence, just as the "wisdom of God" *(sophia)* was depicted as a woman at work in the world (Proverbs 8).

Logos in Greek Thought

But John's audience was not just exposed to Jewish thinking. They lived in a world infused with Greek philosophy and thought. For the Greeks, the term *Logos* also described an activity and had also taken on a life of its own. It was the divine principle of reason that gave order to the universe and linked the human mind with the mind of God.

The Jewish philosopher Philo (20 B.C.–A.D.50), trying to harmonize Hebrew and Greek worlds of thought, had pulled these two concepts together and had used the term *Logos* to talk about an

■ In what way does the concept of *Logos* differ from your previous ideas about "the Word"? What does it mean? How does it describe God?

■ What is the difference, if any, between the *Logos* as a description of God's activity in Jesus and saying Jesus is the *Logos*?

entity that mediated between God and the world as divine creativity and revelation. The concept was therefore in the language of John's community. What was different, and shocking for some, was to say that, in some way, this divine principle, this creating, revealing activity of God, had somehow entered human history in a man called Jesus.

God as <u>Logos</u> in the World

▼ Let's listen to what John says. Just as physical light came into being in creation through the *Logos* as the creating, speaking activity of God, dispelling the darkness of the uncreated void, so this same *Logos* has acted again, bringing spiritual light into the spiritual darkness of the world through this man Jesus (John 1:1-9). Physical light gave life at creation; this "spiritual" light will give spiritual life to all people, a light that the darkness can never overtake (1:3-5). Thus John has introduced his plot: God at work (Logos) in the world.

It is vitally important we follow John's story as he wants to tell it. We are so used to mixing all the Gospels together, adding some theological ideas from the fourth-century creeds, and stirring! However, that is not what John was doing. He was following a very specific argument for his community so as to help them think through their relationship to God—being God's children—now that they no longer had the synagogue heritage to draw upon.

We also have to be careful not to think John is dealing with the questions about Jesus that arose some two centuries later. When John says that this *Logos* "became flesh and lived among us" (1:14), he is not saying God equals Jesus. ◆ This equation would absorb the fourth-century church: whether and how a man could be, at the same time, both a human being and a divine being and, if so, whether this human-divine Jesus was as divine as God or a lesser-level divinity.

Such questions would not even occur to John's audience on hearing the word *Logos* because they

---

▼ How do the images of light and darkness describe the state of the world for you? the state of the spirit?

◆ Understanding the doctrine of the Trinity, developed later in the church to describe the relationship between God, Jesus, and the Holy Spirit, can be confusing. John does not equate Jesus with God. How do you describe this relationship? What does it mean to your relationship with God?

would know John was referring to the activity of God in the world, just as God had always been described in Hebrew thinking. They might be outside the synagogue, and John might be helping them redefine themselves, but the way they thought was still embedded in the culture of their background and experience. *Logos* was a description of God's activity in the world, but the new and enthralling thought was that, somehow, the God that had "spoken" in Hebrew history by revealing and creating, was now speaking to them in a new location—the man Jesus whom they followed.

The Story Within the Story

Paul concentrated on the events after Easter: the risen Christ he encountered on the road to Damascus and the Spirit that inspired the body of Christ, the church. He spent little time describing the life of Jesus and his disciples. The Synoptic Gospels concentrated on what happened before Easter: a Jewish man who talked about a coming reign of God, died for it, and was finally declared, through the Resurrection, the Messiah, the "one sent."

● John treads a different path, holding together two stories from the beginning. As we have seen, the larger story is the cosmic story of the *Logos*—God's activity in the world from the beginning. Within this large story, the heavenly story (3:12), is a specific "earthly" story, a circle within the big circle—"God at work" in the man Jesus. At every moment in John's Gospel these two stories are being told, sharing the same space "in the flesh." To make sense of John then, both stories have to be kept in our minds as we read each verse, in order to see which story John is telling in which moment—a real challenge at times!

● John tackles the "Jesus story" from both dimensions: "God at work" before and after Easter. Do you think John succeeds in holding the two stories together, a human story within a larger cosmic story? How is this helpful (or unhelpful) to you for reading John? How do the stories work together for you to invite you to a life of discipleship now and forever with God?

● By John inviting us into his story with explanatory asides of the events going on, does this also invite you into a response to believe or not to believe? Why do you think some people believed and some did not? Does John give us any clues?

Signs Tell the Story

John arranges the first part of his Gospel (Chapters 1–12) as a series of signs (miracles) done by Jesus. With each sign, the invitation is "come and see." The first "seeing" is always the human story: watching the miraculous act and interpreting it in human categories. "Who is this man that can do these things? How does he do it?"

We, the readers, know there is another encounter going on—the encounter with the *Logos*, "God at work" in the world. We watch to see if the one seeing the sign will simply read it as the work of a Jewish miracle worker or will see it and believe it to be "God at work" in the world, the larger story. The double layer of the story is patently obvious to us readers because of the way John tells the stories.

It is as if he takes us up on a rooftop so we can see the cosmic layout, while the humans below struggle to understand from their earthly view. We despair at the constant misunderstandings of what Jesus says and does because we know the bigger story from the start and don't have to figure it out as the signs multiply and events unfold.

▲ Each sign—changing the water to wine (2: 1-11), curing the royal official's son (4:46-54), curing the paralyzed man at the Bethzatha (Bethesda or Bethsaida) pool (5:1-18), multiplying the loaves and fishes (6:1-14), walking on water (6:16-21), healing the blind man (9:1-41), raising Lazarus (11:1-44)—is described in dramatic detail. These signs give Jesus an opportunity to entice the audience from their absorption with the earthly details toward the heavenly meaning, the larger story they are also encountering of "God at work."

While we see clearly the dou-

▲ In small groups, look up each of the signs. What happened? What are the differences between the signs? the similarities? Who was influenced directly and how? Who was influenced indirectly? What importance do these signs have today? for you?

▼ Look now at the conclusions drawn by the initial observers of the signs. Read the passages. Try to imagine how you might have reacted to the sign you looked up if you were an initial observer. How do you think you would have felt? If you saw a similar event today at the mall or the marketplace, what would you think? What if it happened at church? What do you think about miracles today as signs of God's activity in the world? How do you define a "miracle"?

ble meanings in Jesus' words, especially with the help of John's editorial comments, the hearers struggle to understand. ▼ They are absorbed in Jewish expectations; and their conclusions roam from whether Jesus is a miracle worker (2:1-12), a new teacher sent from God (3:1-3), a new prophet (4:16-19; 7:45-52), the expected Messiah and Son of God appointed to fulfill Jewish (3:25-30; 7:40-44) and even Samaritan (4: 25-26) hopes, to a troublemaker and insurrectionist (7:40-46; 12:9-11, 19), or a charlatan (6:60-66; 9:13-41).

Confusion!

◆ Nicodemus cannot understand why his simple question "Are you a teacher from God?" has turned into a confusing discussion about being born again "from above" of water and Spirit (3:4-8). The Samaritan woman, who makes considerably more progress in understanding than Nicodemus, is confused as to where Jesus can get living (running) water instead of well water (4:7-15). The disciples cannot understand how Jesus obtained food they don't know about—did someone slip him a snack without their knowledge (4:31-34)? The Pharisees who see the lame man walk become embroiled in an argument as to whether it is lawful for him to carry his mat on the sabbath (5:8-11). The parents of the blind man, even though they know their son was blind from birth, won't even talk about his healing for fear of what might happen to them (9:19-23). Even the night before Jesus' death, when the disciples finally think they get it, Jesus shows them they still don't understand, and their actions will soon demonstrate that this is true (16:29-32; 18:10-11, 15-27).

The Plot Thickens

● As the signs accelerate through John, two lists begin to form: those who understand, believe, and know, and those who don't

◆ Review the passages about the confusion some of these persons experienced, starting with Nicodemus. We have the benefit of centuries of hindsight, but they didn't. Why were they confused? Would the cumulation of these signs help you believe, do you think, or compound confusion?

● Review the story of the raising of Lazarus (John 11:1-44) if you need to, and then pay particular attention to the reaction of "the Jews" (11:45-53). What different ways did they respond? What were the arguments at the Council meeting?

understand, believe, or know. There is always a gap in the middle where some hesitate, not quite declaring, or going back and forth depending on the circumstances. Yet other people have gone beyond simply not believing and are determined to do away with this man causing trouble in their midst. Their anger, slowly building over many chapters, explodes with the final sign, the raising of Lazarus (11:28-44). Before we know it, we are hurtling down the hill toward the death of Jesus, gathering momentum with each verse. Yet somehow, because there are two stories going, there is a strong sense that we are not headed for disaster and tragedy, but glory. What has happened? According to John, Jesus' hour, which we are told about in the very first sign (2:4; 12:23), has come!

The Hour Has Come!

From this moment on, the direction of John's two stories changes. The raising of Lazarus was the last straw for Jesus' opponents. Crowds were flocking to Jesus because of the signs, and the chief priests and Pharisees feared this might upset the Romans and bring on an attack. Better one man die than the Jewish nation be destroyed, they reasoned. From then on, they resolved to put Jesus to death, to end the human story (11:45-53).

■ In our larger story, however, the raising of Lazarus gave opportunity for the totality of God's message to the world to be revealed. Those who believe in God's commitment to be in relationship with humanity, communicated through Jesus' work and words, have entered already into life with the Eternal that will not be interrupted by physical death (11:23-26). God's work in Jesus has now been completed, and, as Jesus is lifted up at the end of his life, the glory of God will be fully revealed (12:27-32).

In the Synoptic Gospels, tragedy compounds as Jesus is dragged inevitably closer to his cruel death. Darkness encompasses the earth as a sign that the powers of darkness seem to have

■ Do you think the priests and the Pharisees had a reasonable point in being worried that unruly crowds around Jesus might fuel Roman attacks on the Jews? If you had been one of the leaders (and therefore, protectors) of the Jewish religious society, what might you have done?

■ Have you ever had cherished faith beliefs challenged? Did you stand up for your faith? ignore the challenge? give up? If you experienced the same thing again, how would you apply what you learned from your first experience?

won, and we must wait for the Resurrection to hear evidence to the contrary: "He has been raised; he is not here!" (Mark 16:6; Matthew 28:6-7; Luke 24:5). In John, however, the human story of the tragedy of Jesus' death is eclipsed by the triumphant completion of God's work in the world, a work not just centered around Jesus' death and resurrection, but encompassing the whole of Jesus' life and ministry as the incarnation of God at work in the world. The end of Jesus' life made God's invitation to humanity to be in an eternal relationship, offered by Jesus throughout his life, available to all who believe it (John 3:16; 12:27-33).

▲ Thus, through the betrayal, trial, and crucifixion of Jesus, we do not see the Synoptic Jesus who prays in agony in the garden asking, "if it is possible, let this cup pass from me" (Matthew 26:39; Mark 14:36; Luke 22:42). Rather, we see Jesus as one fully aware of what is happening and in control of the events (John 12:27-32).

He chides Peter for drawing his sword—Am I not to drink the cup that the Father has given me? (18:11). He does not stay silent in his arrest and trial. Instead, the interrogators become the interrogated (18:19-24) and the judges are put on trial (19:1-16). Jesus himself orchestrates his end. ▼ In John's eloquent description of Jesus' last moments "lifted up" on the cross, both stories become one as Jesus says, "It is finished"—the work of a man appointed by God for a task and the task of the Incarnate *Logos* in the world (19:30).

God's Work Never Stops

◆ The story of Jesus the man ends for John when the man dies, but the story of "God at work" in the world does not. It is obvious from John's stories that the appearances to the disciples after Jesus' death were not the human (born of the flesh) Jesus back again. They did not recognize him as the one they knew until he spoke (20:14-17, 19-20, 26).

▲ Look up the Passion narratives. (Use a parallel Bible if you have one.) What does John mean by "the hour has come"? How does this hour differ from the way the Synoptic Gospels report it?

▼ What do you think John's image of eternal life is? Is this different from yours?

◆ How would you describe the work of the Father that Jesus saw himself sent to do (John 5:16-17, 19-20)?

What they then experienced with certainty was that the life of abiding in God they had shared with Jesus on earth had not been destroyed by death. While Jesus was no longer with them in the flesh, the *Logos* that had been at work in him was now in them as a community, together with the commission to do the work that had been Jesus' human task (20:21-23). They were now the human story of "God at work"— the story of a loving relationship with the Eternal. This human story would be replayed again and again in successive communities who believe that they are the household of God, the place where God dwells and works in the world (14:15-21).

The Divine Relationship

● We are left in no doubt about the joy of living and abiding in love with the Eternal and each other after reading chapters 13–17. These chapters contain some of the most beautiful imagery and language about what it means to be in relationship with God, to know God, and to be known by God. Through evocative metaphors of a network of love (13:31-35), of family (14:1-31), of the vine and branches (15:1-11), of the joy of childbirth after labor (16:21-24), of protection and sanctuary against the world (17:11-19), and of privileged knowledge of the divine (15:7-11), John has assured his readers of what is reserved for those who believe and understand. This stands in sharp contrast to those who don't and who, by the end of John's story, have become synonymous with "the Jews" (1:10-11; 3:10-12; 5:18-25; 10:25-30; 15:18-25), something we have to deal with as twenty-first–century Christians. ■ This was the good news for the Johannine community.

● In small groups, study these six passages about what it means to be in relationship with God. What does the image or message tell you about God? about Jesus? about God's relationship with humanity? Can you identify yourself as someone Jesus is speaking to in these passages? What draws you in or keeps you from feeling a part?

■ How have the Scriptures covered in this session been good news for you? Through the imagery of the vine and the branches, Jesus said, "Abide in me as I abide in you" (15:4). Close in prayer, making your own response, if you wish, to this invitation from Jesus to be part of the household of God.

3

JOHN DIAGNOSES THE HUMAN CONDITION

John in a nutshell is the story of the healing of the blind man (John 9). ▲ Every recurring theme and layer of understanding are there. John, artist par excellence, produces a canvas not only of human events, but also of the cosmic story of God.

Jesus and the Blind Man

▼ Jesus and his disciples encounter a man who had been blind from birth. This prompts a question from the disciples, "Rabbi, who sinned?" (9:2). There was speculation at the time that, if someone was born blind, it was because he or she had sinned in the womb or the parents had sinned. The disciples obviously knew this debate and were curious to see where their teacher stood. Jesus dismissed the question—physical blindness has nothing to do with anyone's sin (see Ezekiel 18:1-4, 20).

We miss the point, like the disciples did many times, if we read Jesus' following comments to suggest that the man's blindness was planned simply to demonstrate God's point in this moment. Such an understanding is out of character for the compassionate God we meet in John. Rather, as with every sign in John, the existing human situation provided a jumping off point for the larger story of "God at work." When Jesus says the man was born blind "so that God's works might be revealed in him," John is already in the larger

▲ What way do you learn best? Do you find it easier to understand a theological point if it is described in a story or painted as a picture?

▼ Read Ezekiel 18:1-4, 20 and reread John 9:1-3. What do you think of the argument that God causes or allows physical incapacity or illnesses for a purpose? Do you think this is what Jesus meant in talking about the man's blindness? Do you think Jesus says anything about the cause of the man's blindness in this story? Explain.

story. He is not commenting on why this man is blind, but on the opportunity it provides to see "God at work" (9:4-5).

The healing unfolds. Jesus spreads mud paste on the man's eyes and sends him to wash in the pool of Siloam. When the man returns, he can see. As different groups of people react to the healing, the blind man emerges as a wonderful character, sticking to his story regardless of opposition—"One thing I do know, that though I was blind, now I see" (9:25). John's readers know what the observers of the miracle don't—the man's reply is the perfect response to the good news in the larger story of "God at work."

◆ Despite the healed man's insistence that he is the man born blind, neighbors and friends don't believe it. The Pharisees interrogate the man endlessly. They don't believe him because Jesus healed on the sabbath, and God would not work through a sinner. They ask the man's parents if he really was blind from birth; but the parents, afraid they will be put out of the synagogue, tell the Pharisees to ask their son instead! The Pharisees then command the healed man to give glory to God, not this "sinner" Jesus, for his healing. We readers know what delicious irony this is. The healed man stands firm, not corroborating any accusations against Jesus. He even gets testy, telling them he has no idea if Jesus is a sinner or not. All he knows is that he was once blind, but now can see.

● The Pharisees try a different tactic. They ask, not whether Jesus did it, but how. Our healed man turns the question on them, suggesting their intense interest means they want to be Jesus' disciples too!

That did it! The Pharisees revile him, accusing him of being a disciple of Jesus while they are disciples of Moses. Everyone knows God spoke through Moses, but no one even knows where Jesus came from. It is not the miracle that concerns the Pharisees, but the authority with which it was done.

The man makes his final point to those who were supposed to know everything: "God doesn't

◆ With which spectator do you most identify in this story? What would your concerns be if confronted with such a miracle today? What do the reactions of the onlookers tell you about your own faith?

● Can you see parallels between the concerns of the Pharisees about sticking by religious rules and some of our institutional concerns as churches today? What do you think Jesus would say to our concerns?

listen to sinners, but does listen to those who worship and obey him. I am cured. This man did it. Therefore, he must be from God!"

■ The Pharisees cannot fault the man's logic, so they attack his credentials, calling him a sinner. It is clear what they thought about the origins of blindness! They drive him away.

When Jesus hears, he finds the man and asks if he believes in the Son of Man. The man hears it as a human question. He had not heard of this person, but his faith in Jesus is such that he requests more information so he might believe. Jesus replies from the larger story, "You have 'seen' him. The one speaking with you is he."

A Model of Belief

▲ This man is John's model for those who encounter Jesus. He heard Jesus speak, saw Jesus act, and believed. Jesus explains the bigger picture to him—those who do not see will see; those who do see remain blind. Eavesdropping on this conversation, the Pharisees laugh, "So he thinks people who can see will become blind, eh?" They don't know the larger conversation taking place.

Jesus confounds them with his reply: "If you were blind, you would not have sin. But now that you say, 'We see,' your sin remains" (9:41). The reader knows that, in God's story, sin is not ritual impurity or disobeying Jewish law. It is "not believing." If the Pharisees were blind, that is, had not encountered Jesus, they could not be charged with unbelief. Once, however, they "see" Jesus and do not believe, they proclaim their unbelief, and thus are sinners (15:22-24).

The Irony of "Seeing"

▼ It would take a whole book to enjoy all the twists and turns, the irony and double meaning, the

■ Do you have experience with someone (yourself?) holding on to old thinking, even when presented with an obvious and new way to assess a situation or attitude? What, generally, is the effect? What are the risks of believing in new ways? What are the effects on your faith and spiritual growth?

▲ What exactly is it, in the larger story that the observers were being asked to believe about Jesus and about God? Are there ways that illness and sin are related? What Scripture supports your response?

▼ What do you think of John's definition of *sin* as "not believing"? Do you think this covers sin adequately?

interplay between characters in this wonderful story. The Pharisees call Jesus a sinner because he doesn't follow God's rules, yet Jesus calls them sinners because they do not believe God is at work in him.

Those who make a living knowing the law do not understand, while those with no credentials know through their experience. Those who have perfect sight and ample opportunity to understand are blind to "God at work," while the sightless see a man from God. The Pharisees debate Jesus' credentials, while we readers know Jesus has the highest of credentials! The healed man accepts the simplest credential of all—it worked!

◆ The Johannine community would identify with many characters in this story. Exclusion from the synagogue was a reality, so the parents' fears would be understood, especially by those remaining in the synagogue as secret Christians (7:10-13; 19:38).

The sheer bravery of the healed man would come across as a lesson in true discipleship. No matter how much the Pharisees grilled him or declared him unworthy in order to get him to renounce his claims, he stood firm, defending the one thing he knew to be true. When Jesus revealed the larger story of "God at work" to him, he said without hesitation, "Lord, I believe."

The Human Condition Diagnosed

● We must drag ourselves away from John's magnificent storytelling to ask what we can learn about John's diagnosis of the human condition. From John we can expect answers on different levels, but there is one overarching cosmic theme into which all others fit—light and darkness.

How large is cosmic? The very first act of the *Logos* in the beginning was to bring light into being, transforming the formless void

---

◆ Who do you think the parents might represent in our day? Read John 7:10-13; 19:38, concerning secret believers. Why, do you think, were these persons afraid to confess their belief? Have you ever had conviction, but not courage? If folk believe because they encounter Jesus, either in the flesh as these people did, or through the witness of a loving community, what does this say to us about being disciples?

● How would you describe a life of "darkness" without God today: (a) the "darkness" of not knowing about God's love, or (b) the "darkness" of refusing to believe God's love? Explain. Is there a more appropriate and expressive metaphor for unbelief in the twenty-first century? Explain.

and darkness covering the deep (Genesis 1:1-3). When God saw this light was good, God separated light from darkness (Genesis 1:4-5). This is the story of how physical light came into being by the *Logos,* but there is a larger story. Through this same *Logos,* the spiritual Light that enlightens everyone has come into the world (John 1:8-9). This Light shines in the darkness, and the darkness cannot overcome it (1:5).

■ The suggestion of darkness struggling against light gives the clue to the human condition:

> And this is the judgment, that the light has come into the world, and people loved darkness rather than light because their deeds were evil. For all who do evil hate the light and do not come to the light, so that their deeds may not be exposed. But those who do what is true come to the light, so that it may be clearly seen that their deeds have been done in God (3:19-21).

My mother still reminds me that, as a child, when I went down the external stairs of our house at night, to put out the garbage or get something stored underneath the house, I whistled loudly all the way. (This was in Brisbane, Australia, where houses are built on high posts with space underneath.) I was afraid of the dark and figured that, if for any reason I stopped whistling, someone would come looking for me! It was not that it was night—I loved the night stars if someone was with me. It was because I couldn't see, and therefore couldn't know if something dangerous or frightening lurked somewhere nearby.

Human Darkness

▲ When John suggests to his readers that being in darkness is the human problem, a host of images would come to their minds. Darkness was a familiar metaphor in the ancient Near East. In relation to human beings, it could mean something as normal as physical death (Psalm

■ Read John 3:19-21 and this personal anecdote about whistling in the dark. Is the encounter with "God at work" in the world a one-time event, or is it more of an ongoing process? How would you describe encountering God in your life? Are you ever afraid you will encounter God? If so, why?

▲ Look up several of the Scripture passages that mention darkness in the two paragraphs describing the earthly and cosmic dimensions of darkness. How is the image used? How does it illustrate for you what it means to live in God's love?

88:9-12), innocent ignorance or being in the dark (Genesis 32:22-32), or plain foolishness (Ecclesiastes 2:13-14). Darkness also represented a whole range of negative experiences: evil (Matthew 6:22-23; Acts 26:17-18), terror (Genesis 15:12; Isaiah 5:30; Psalm 35:6; 91:5-6), despair (Psalm 143:3), punishment (Deuteronomy 28:28-29; Proverbs 20:20), alienation or lostness (1 John 1:6-7; 2:8-11), exclusion (Isaiah 47:5), and destruction (Matthew 24:15-29).

In the cosmic arena, darkness was anything opposed to, or the opposite of, God, the giver of life and light (Proverbs 4:18-19). It could simply be the human inability to look on divine glory (Deuteronomy 5:22; Psalm 97:2), it could be God's opposition to evil (Exodus 10:21-23; Mark 15:33; Ephesians 5:6-14), or it could be death as eternal punishment (Matthew 8:12).

For ancient Israel, *sheol* (Hell) was darkness—a netherworld of departed spirits (Job 17:13-16). It may surprise you, but ancient Israel originally had no belief in survival or in life after death. We first hear of death being overcome in some way in Daniel 12:1-2, a sixth-century B.C. story written down around 175 B.C. Although Sheol as punishment is hinted at in Isaiah 66:24, it did not become a place of eternal punishment in Jewish tradition until the third century B.C.

Whichever meaning is intended when the metaphor of darkness is used, one thing is sure. The reality everyone experiences about darkness is that, once a candle is lit or a light turned on, darkness cannot be sustained unless there is a deliberate attempt to remove, hide, or walk away from the light (Psalm 119:105; Luke 15:8-10). In the cosmic realm therefore, when God the Light comes, darkness cannot exist in the same space (John 1:3-5). As the psalmist said: "Even the darkness is not dark to you; / the night is as bright as the day, / for darkness is as light to you" (Psalm 139:12).

Because of this truth, the coming of the Light (Zechariah 14:7; Isaiah 9:2; Matthew 4:16) is also a dark day, because it forces a choice—to reject the light (by turning away from it into darkness), or by hiding from it (loving darkness better than light [Joel 2:2; Amos 5:18]).

▼ Do you think John is suggesting that, once people come to the light, they are always in the light; or do people go back and forth— believing and not believing?

Darkness and Blindness

▼ Drawing on this wealth of imagery, John calls the human condition darkness, as opposed to being in the light; blindness as opposed to seeing. But there are two types of darkness in John that must not be rolled together— darkness (blindness) as a natural condition, the innocent ignorance of light; and darkness as a choice, choosing darkness or blindness after experiencing light.

The blind man is in darkness because he cannot see. Jesus makes it very clear to his disciples that his blindness has nothing to do with evil or sin. The human situation is simply that he was born blind, end of story. He is also in the dark because he does not know who Jesus is when Jesus confronts him. He does not initiate the miracle because he does not know Jesus is able to heal. After the healing, he still doesn't know Jesus' credentials or from where he appeared.

What he does know, however, from his experience of the encounter, is that somehow he can see—the best proof of all! He was not healed because he was out looking for a miracle, or because he believed in Jesus' power ahead of time and asked for healing. In fact, being blind from birth meant he did not even know what he was missing! Darkness has no meaning (like the void of Genesis 1:1) until we have seen the light. It is only when Jesus finds him and heals him that the man knows from experience that he was previously in darkness.

Finding the Light of God

This wonderful human story sets the scene for the larger story of blindness or darkness—life without the Light of God. The blind man represents everyone who has not yet encountered the Light of God. This initial darkness is the human condition—it has nothing to do with knowing you are in darkness, or sinful, or even seeking out the light, because we do not know what the Light of God is until we encounter it. Only then do we know about darkness.

We do not encounter the Light because of our faith, but the Light encounters us. Faith came for the blind man only in the slow realization of the reality of his experience. Even when Jesus sought him out to tell him the bigger story, the man's faith did not come from his understanding of who Jesus, the Son of Man was, but through his experience—once he was in darkness, now he is in the Light.

This human condition of darkness for John, therefore, prior to encountering Light, is not the awareness of sin and the need for salvation. It is not having yet heard the invitation scattered throughout John—"come and see" (1:38-39, 41-42, 46, 50; 4:28-30; and so on).

Seeing Without Believing

◆ John describes a second type of darkness that is also part of the human condition. The blind man believed in Jesus because of his experience (9:35-41) and chose to enter into a relationship with the Light (1:5). The neighbors and the Pharisees, however, also encountered God through this healing; but, even though they saw what happened, they did not "see" or encounter the larger significance of "God at work."

In their moment of decision, they chose to reject the Light come into the world in Jesus (3:19-21; 8:12), turning away to walk into the darkness. This was a choice, because once the Light has been seen, to hide from it or turn away is to choose not to live in the Light. This choice for darkness (not to believe) is sin (9:41). In the darkness without the light, all things die.

● John reminds us of these two different types of darkness time and time again with words he chooses for what seems unnecessary detail in his storytelling. Nicodemus comes to Jesus by night (3:1-2). This is not something sinister, nor his realization that he is a sinner. He is an honest inquirer who has heard of Jesus and "comes to see." On the other hand, Judas, who has been with Jesus and has had ample time to experience living in the Light, chooses to go out into the night (see 13:30).

Choosing Light or Darkness

■ The variety of people John describes who see the healing yet balk at believing, tells us there are many reasons people choose not to believe but to remain in darkness. For the blind man, it was easy. He knew through experience that God was at work and believed without further discussion. The neighbors did not believe because they simply could not accept the evidence given. The Pharisees did not believe at first because Jesus had not followed their religious rules. When

◆ Who do you know who best lives in the light? What have you learned from this person?

● Who is the most honest inquirer you know? What have you learned from this person?

■ Does the story of the blind man suggest new ways for you to live in the world?

JOHN'S MESSAGE

the parents would not support the Pharisees' preconceived ideas against the evidence, they tried fear tactics on the man, finally justifying their unbelief by calling both the man and Jesus sinners, negating the evidence.

The parents, despite every reason to believe and rejoice in their son's healing, refused to commit themselves for fear of the consequences. Their not taking a stand was a choice for darkness because they hid from the light. The reality of the human condition, John says, is that, given the choice, many love darkness rather than light because of their own motives and agendas.

A Moment of Judgment

▲ For John, the decision to believe in Jesus brings the believer into life in the Light at that moment. The decision not to believe is the moment of judgment, the beginning of death in this world, where death is living without the Light. While darkness as the human condition begins as innocent ignorance of what light means, once light is encountered, a decision must be made. A decision to turn from the light loses its innocence and becomes the way of death—separated from God's love, alienated, orphaned, adrift, deprived of sustenance, in danger from the evil one in the world (17:15).

▼ John does not spell out this darkness in graphic detail; rather he describes the opposite—the joy of life abiding in the love of God (15:1-11). Only as we experience God's love do we know what it is not to be loved. Only as we experience being children of God can we imagine what it is like to be orphans. The invitation to believe in John is not born of fear or despair, but is "come and see," because the power of God is such that in the seeing is the believing. Thus it was in Jesus' day. So it still is when people encounter the love of God, shown in Jesus and now modeled in loving communities living in the Light (12:35-36). It is not surprising that *enlightening* was a term for baptism in the early church—coming to the Light.

▲ Discuss, from your experience, how metaphors of light and darkness have been applied in harmful ways to people or groups. Is it still possible to use such metaphors? What other metaphors or images would be more helpful for the twenty-first century?

▼ Have you ever felt outside of God's family? Jesus promised that the Spirit of truth would continue to urge us to "come and see." Take time, if you wish, to respond to this invitation. Close with prayer.

While *darkness* and *light* offered a wealth of meaning for John's audience, they are troubling images for the twenty-first century. Our memory of centuries where *dark, black, evil, ignorant, inferior,* even *nonhuman,* were associated with dark skin color, as opposed to *light, white, good, civilized, superior, fully human* being associated with the white, European race can get in the way. Missionaries and colonizers spoke of "darkest Africa" and the "blindness" of non-Christian religions, especially in primal cultures. Such racist overtones are difficult to erase when we hear John's message, especially if we have been victims of such imagery. Twenty-first–century Christians must ask whether such descriptions can still be used, and if not, what new images describe more justly and adequately what John meant about the transformatory encounter with Jesus.

JOHN TELLS US ABOUT JESUS CHRIST

I remember how a church school teacher explained Jesus to me when I was a child. She said, "If you wanted to tell a colony of ants that you loved them and wanted to be their friend and protector, how would you do it?" Of course, the answer was, "Become an ant." Another ant can show and tell a message from another source because an ant knows ant language. Also an ant can demonstrate love for another ant far better than a human-ant encounter, which would inevitably end up in a squished ant situation! ◆

Getting the Point Across

Children get that picture easily because they are used to books where animals speak like humans, and humans turn into all sorts of things for the purpose of the story. The problem comes when adults get hold of such a description. Instead of seeing it as a story of how to communicate across incompatible borders—ant and human realms, for instance— they get hung up in debates about whether and how a human could become an ant, forgetting the original point of the story: the job of sending a message.

● This situation reminds me a little of someone trying to explain to me how faxes and e-mails work. I am sure there is a good explanation, but I have yet to find it. However, I am utterly convinced that faxes and e-mails are

---

◆ What are images for God and Jesus that you remember from your childhood church school days? Which were helpful and which were not helpful? Explain.

● What things in life do you take on faith without knowing how or why they work? Is there a difference when it comes to religious beliefs? How integral are the central theological ideas (Incarnation, Crucifixion, virgin birth, Son of God, and so on) to your faith journey? Explain.

the most wonderful way to keep in touch with my family and friends when oceans of water and miles of air-space separate us. I will leave the solution of how it happens to those who create the machines and keep them running, while I enjoy the benefits.

The blind man in our last chapter was like this. He had no idea how Jesus healed him or even who Jesus was. That did not matter in the grand scheme of things. What mattered was that, through this man, Jesus, he received his sight. The proof was in the results. Even when Jesus tried to explain to him who had healed him, and how this was possible, the man still did not much care. He was willing to let Jesus worry about that. He simply believed something happened because it worked!

I think this is where we have problems in the church with the idea of Jesus. The message of the Gospels in their Jewish setting is about God communicating with humankind, something that had happened from the beginning of history and now had happened through this man, Jesus. However, somewhere along the way, we became more concerned with how this could have happened than with celebrating that it did.

▲ Theologians have long used the phrase "the person and work of Christ" to study the meaning of Jesus. It seems our discussions revolve around who Jesus was in relation to God—was he divine and in what way? We have allowed this to explain Jesus, rather than talking about what we can know from human experience—what Jesus did—and allowing that to tell us about his relationship to God.

Sharing a Task

John concentrates on what Jesus did by telling us two separate stories that overlap and that also have lives of their own. When we allow John's two stories to tell themselves and listen to what links them together, we get a surprise. The shared point between the story of the man, Jesus, and the larger story of God is a common task, or work as Jesus calls it. What is this work that is, at the same time, the work of God and the work of Jesus?

This work is to communicate God's desire to be in a relationship of love with human beings, not affected by physical death. Not only was this message told by

▲ What do you think is the difference between discussing the person and discussing the work of Jesus? How would you describe the work of Jesus? How would you describe the work of God? How do they differ?

Jesus, it was also demonstrated in Jesus' love for his followers, even to the point of dying rather than reneging on the task.

The Human Story

▼ The human story is the story of Jesus, a Jewish man sent to do a task. This concept was not new to the Jews. Their history was littered with prophets, kings, and wise men sent by God for specific tasks among the people. The Jewish expectation of a messiah was of one sent from God to do something. They only disagreed as to what they expected this person to do for them.

The Sadducees, the aristocratic ruling class—the Establishment in our terms—were political. They had control of the Temple and its offices, negotiated with the Romans, and held the Torah to be adequate for all their needs. It is not very clear what they would have wanted in a messiah.

The Pharisees kept the Jews faithful to the Law through their teachings and rule-setting. Their vision of a messiah was probably a religious leader or teacher who would perfectly observe the Law and thus lead the people to repent of their evil ways.

The Essenes, a group of disenchanted visionaries who retreated to the desert to live a separate and pure life, wanted a messiah who would defeat the Romans and establish a messianic kingdom on earth. The Zealots, on the other hand, were a band of revolutionaries whose chief desire was to lead a revolt against the Romans—guerrilla soldiers organizing for the moment when a warrior-king messiah would lead them in their revolt. When that messiah still did not come, they formed their own revolution that resulted in the Jewish wars of A.D. 70.

Is Jesus the Messiah?

◆ With this variety of meanings around the word *messiah*, no wonder everyone was keen to see whether Jesus was this leader. When we look at their expectations, however, we see that none

▼ Using a Bible dictionary, look up *Messiah*. Then look up *Sadducess, Pharisees, Essenes,* and *Zealots* to see if there is added information about the expectations each of these groups would have had about the Messiah.

◆ What has been your definition of *Messiah*? Have these lessons clarified your thinking? If so, in what way? What have you learned about the Jewish faith through these studies that you did not appreciate before? about your own faith?

of them expected a messiah to be God. Messiah was to be a man sent by God, called from among the people for a task.

And, let's face it, as in every age, the majority of the Jews probably didn't think too much about it at all! Therefore, when we hear the question from ordinary people and from the Pharisees when they encountered Jesus, "Are you the Messiah sent from God?" it was a straightforward question, not about a person, but about the task he would do for them.

Our larger story is also about God's task or work in the world, as we have already seen. The Jewish people never presumed to pry into the divine mystery of God to somehow discover the mind and will of God. They knew God by what God was doing in their world—God's activity, or, as we saw with the *Logos*, "God at work." Our larger story of "God at work" is not the story of all God is or does. We could never comprehend that as ants, nor could an ant contain the entire cosmic story. Rather, it is the story of "God at work" in our history, the "ant-phase" of God's career as it were.

This story of God's work began for the Hebrew people at Creation, continued in God sending Abraham from Ur to the Promised Land, accelerated with God's delivery of the people from slavery in Egypt, and grated like a broken record in the constant breaking of the covenant and its restoration. It is within this history of God's work from the beginning that we have to understand God's work in Jesus.

● In this context of Jewish history, Jesus was the Anointed One, a chosen emissary sent to the world from among the people for a task—to show and tell that God is at work in him, communicating a message of God's love. Jesus' work was God's work.

There may be two stories, the story of "God at work" and the story of "Jesus at work," but the unity and oneness is a unity of task ("the Father and I are one") in the work of God in the world (10:22-30). Jesus has no other task than this. John makes it very clear that this is what Jesus claims—to do the work of the God who sent him (4:34; 5:16-17, 19-20, 30, 36; 6:28-32; 9:4; 10:24-26, 37-38; 12:49; 14:10-

● Choose from among these many references about the work of God Jesus was sent to do. What do they tell you about God's work and Jesus' task? How do they call you to perceive your own work for God, both what you do and what you say? What motivates and empowers you for such work?

12; 17:4-8; and so on). And, just as Jesus was anointed, appointed, and sent by God to do God's work, so Jesus' followers also receive the Spirit to help them in their role as anointed, appointed, and sent ones, continuing God's work in the world (14:8-12; 15:26-27; 17:18).

Working on the Sabbath

■ The story of Jesus healing the sick man at the pool of Bethzatha (sometimes spelled Bethesda or Bethsaida) (5:1-30) spells out how Jesus saw himself in relation to God. The Pharisees had objected, not to his healing the man, but because Jesus was working on the sabbath, the same objection they had to the healing of the blind man (9:16).

▲ The Pharisees taught that people should rest on the sabbath, as God had done after Creation. Jesus argued that if his Father rested on every sabbath, life would cease; and, since the Father was working, so must the Son, who does the same work as the Father (5:17). The Jews attacked Jesus at this point, not only for breaking the sabbath but also for claiming God as his Father, making himself equal to God (5:18). This was a high offense in a religion that was strictly monotheistic (worshiping only one God).

▼ However, in accordance with the pattern throughout John, the Pharisees misunderstood, because they interpreted Jesus' words as the human story, not the larger story of "God at work." How can a human be God? they asked, the same question we often get stuck on. Jesus corrected their misunderstanding by pointing

■ Describe the teachings in your family about the sabbath (Sunday) and how that should be celebrated.

▲ Read John 5:1-13. What are the parallels with the healing of the man born blind (John 9)? What is unique about the story? What was life like for the lame man before he was healed? after? What deep implications are in the story about how the man's life was transformed? Have you ever had a transformational moment with Christ? What was it like, and what have been the results? What message do you get from these stories in John about the point of the sabbath?

▼ How would you describe the relationship between God and Jesus? How would you discuss their work and identity, and that of the Spirit, in your own words? How would you describe this in terms of a doctrine of the Trinity or a triune God? Is the doctrine of the Trinity helpful to you? Explain.

out that he was not talking about being God but being in the same line of work as the Father—the same family business as it were.

The Son, as one given the Father's task to do, does not do anything except what he sees the Father doing. By the same token, the Son can do anything the Father can do because it is "God at work" through him (5:19-21). The works the Son does are the evidence that the Son was appointed, sent as an emissary by the Father for the job (5:36).

Tell Us Plainly

The misunderstanding of the Jews happened again when Jesus was walking in the Temple and the Jews asked him a simple question, "How long will you keep us in suspense? If you are the Messiah, tell us plainly" (10:24). In their encounters with Jesus, he had shown signs of being a Jewish messiah; yet they were not certain. Jesus replied that the many works he has done in the Father's name testify he is sent from God, but they have not believed that "the Father and I are one," that is, sharing the same work (10:29-30).

The Jews misunderstood, thinking again that Jesus was claiming to be God; but Jesus refuted them with their own history. Weren't those in Jewish history to whom the word of God came, or who were consecrated and sent into the world for a task, called gods or sons of God? ◆ Is Jesus therefore blaspheming when he also takes the title Son of God for one doing the works of the Father (10:34-36)?

Furthermore, if his claim of doing God's work is a hurdle for them in coming to belief, he urged them not to believe him, but at least believe the works as "God at work" (10:37-38). These are hardly the words of someone who is trying to make a claim about himself!

Throughout church history, we have tended to misunderstand and to get caught up in the same question the Pharisees did, missing this clarification of the question for us in John. When Jesus talks about the relationship between himself and his Father, he is talking about a shared task. The works Jesus does and the words Jesus says are given him by

---

◆ In what way would you describe Jesus as divine? Explain?

● Examine these Scriptures about "sons of God." Do you have any problems with the language of Father and Son, or other male images in the Scripture? In what way does male language shape our images of God? How would you describe God if a child asked you?

the Father (5:19) as the one appointed or sent to do God's task. In this sense, he is the Jewish Messiah—the sent one that was promised—but, as we will see, the way in which he is the Messiah will surprise all Jewish expectations!

Father and Son: Sharing the Family Business

● What misled the Pharisees was the Father and Son language. This language continues to produce numerous questions in the church. Our task here, however, is to see what John means. It is clear, when we look closely at the context in which John uses these terms, he is not talking about some biological relationship. Jesus calls himself the Son of God, denoting an intimacy of relationship in a task, just as in Hebrew history those appointed by God for proclaiming the word of God or for performing a task for God were called "sons of God."

Israel as a nation is called God's son (Hosea 11:1; Psalm 82:6). Kings as God's anointed were called sons (Psalm 2:7); angels are called sons of God (Job 38:7, Revised Standard Version); and the righteous individual is called a son of God (Wisdom of Solomon 2:18).

■ This idea of a relationship between one sent and the sender standing behind the one sent comes from the Jewish concept of deputy. The officially commissioned envoy or deputy had the authority of the sender and was legally identifiable with the sender. His work carried the authority or bore the name of the one sent. It was a special relationship around a shared purpose; and, in the context of John, the shared purpose is the link between the two stories—the work of binding humans to God and each other in love and commitment (John 17:1-3).

▲ The later church fathers would discuss the titles *Father* and *Son* in the way the Pharisees raised the question: Was Jesus claiming to be God? But this does not fit with the numerous references in John where Jesus makes it clear there is a difference between the Father and the Son—

■ Have you ever considered Jesus' relationship with God as a kind of deputy or emissary? What new insights does that metaphor bring to you? Now read John 17:1-11. How would you describe the relationship Jesus has with humankind? with you?

▲ Can you think of some contemporary image to talk about God—images of communication, love, protection, relationship, and so on?

one addressing the other and standing in relationship with the other.

Addressing the Father and Son

▼ In the imagery of the good shepherd, Jesus is the shepherd, the one with the task of rounding up the sheep into the safety of the fold, the Father's house (10:14-18). In the vine and the branches imagery, Jesus is the vine, doing the work of sustaining the branches, while the vinedresser Father has another task in this shared work (15:1-11).

When Jesus speaks of his death, it is the Father he addresses, indicating they are in the same business of glorifying the name of the Father, but in different ways (12:27-28). ◆ Jesus' long and beautiful prayer addressed to his Father spells out in detail their shared task but different roles (John 17). This shared mission bears the name of the sender, which Jesus also appropriates as the name of his mission (14:13-14). Just as Moses said "I AM" had called and sent him to do God's work in the world (Exodus 3:13-16), so Jesus uses this same name as his authority for doing God's work in the world, saying, "I am the way, the bread, the life, the living water, the truth, the vine," and so forth. ●

The Title Father

As we have done before in this study, it is helpful, in trying to see what John, our great image-maker, means, to look at how the image/title would be heard by his audience. The title *Father* was used sparingly in the Old

---

▼ Read John 10:14-18 and 15:1-11. How would you use these or other images to explain the work of God in the world?

▼ Why has the image of the good shepherd been such a popular image? What does the good shepherd do? Does the metaphor of shepherd lose its strength in a twenty-first–century Western world with little experience of shepherds? What description or illustration would work better, if any, for your personal location and situation? How would you describe how you and Jesus relate?

◆ Read John 17, sometimes referred to as the high priestly prayer. (Use a Bible commentary for more information.) The prayer has three "movements" (17:1-5, 6-19, 20-26). What are those movements? Who or what is Jesus praying for? What does he say about the believers, present and future? Do you see yourself as a subject of this prayer? In what way? What do you believe or hope that the Spirit of Truth wants for you? from you?

Testament for God. When it was, it referred to the role of God as head of the clan or nation, rather than to the fathering role of being a biological parent (Exodus 4:22-23; Hosea 11:1).

■ In the New Testament, *Father* expresses a more personal relationship, modeled on Jesus' relationship with God. Still, this term is within the imagery of a first-century patriarchal household that included servants and relatives who also were fathered or ruled, as well as biological children.

In John's Gospel, the term *Father* is used many, many times more than in any other Gospel, because John is painting a picture of the relationship the Johannine community will have with God, as children of God, in the household of God, not restricted to the Jewish family of God in the synagogue. This relationship as children of the Father is not limited to Jesus alone, but offered to all (John 1:12-13). ▲ Jesus' concern before his death was that they not be left as "orphans" (14:15-18). When the glorified Jesus meets Mary in the garden, he tells her he is going to his Father and her Father (20:17-18), to that intimate relationship of family love saved for all the children of God.

Women and the Father

Some persons find the Father-Son imagery difficult or unsatisfying. One reason some women have found the Father and Son imagery problematic is that it uses a male relationship as the model for the love relationship between God and God's children. Alternative

● Look up Exodus 3:13-16 and the "I am" sayings in John (6:35; 8:12; 9:5; 10:7, 9; 10:11, 14; 11:25-26; 14:6; 15:1, 5). Use a Bible commentary for further exploration, and read the verses surrounding the saying to better understand the context. To whom was Jesus speaking in each instance? How did they respond to his words and self-description? How do we encounter Jesus in the twenty-first century? Be specific!

■ Refer to Exodus 4:22-23 and Hosea 11:1 for some background on the role of God as Father. Then read John 1:12-13. What do these verses mean? Do you refer to God as Father? as Mother? Do you regard yourself as a child of God? Why or why not?

▲ Jesus did not want to leave his followers orphaned. Read John 14:15-31. What assurance does Jesus give his followers? What does *orphaned* mean in this instance? Have you ever felt orphaned from God's parental care? surrounded by God's peace? What assurance do you derive from this passage? What is your source of hope? Explain.

images offered for this relationship have not met with objections from those who read the Father and Son imagery as a *biological* image, rather than an image of a living family relationship. The biological imagery is argued from the Gospels of Matthew and Luke where Mary's pregnancy is attributed to the power of the Holy Spirit.

However, John's Gospel does not have such a birth story, a serious omission if John wanted to argue for a biological link between Father and Son! If John's image of family is about intimate relationships of love, not simply biological relationships, other metaphors can be equally used— parent and child, mother and child, children not servants, friends, workers together with God, to name a few. All these images describe the relationship God offers those who believe: a relationship around a shared task of communicating God's love (17:17-23).

A Wealth of Images

John uses other imagery to talk of this relationship. In the metaphor of the vine (15:1-8), the branches grow and are sustained by their intimate and complete dependence on the vine. The work they jointly do, as branches and vine, is to bear fruit. A branch can only bear fruit by abiding in the vine; if a branch is separated from the vine, it dies. The relationship with God in this image is that of a vine and its branches with God, the vinedresser. In the same way, the imagery of the good shepherd is task-oriented. Jesus is not the sheepfold, but the shepherd, in a shared task of protecting the sheep and offering sanctuary (10:1-18).

▼ This relationship between God and Jesus around a task is also expressed as satisfying hunger with life-sustaining bread (6:22-40), thirst with living water (4:13-14; 7:37-39), and darkness with light for protection and guidance (1:1-4; 8:12-20). All these images from Jewish tradition would give assurance to John's hearers of a continuity in their relationship as people of God (Psalms 80:8-18; 78:70-72; Isaiah 55:1-2; 42:6-7) that does not depend on any biological or lineage ties.

▼ Review these passages about God's relationship with Jesus and Jesus' relationship to John's hearers. How would they assure John's hearers of a continuity in their relationship as a people of God? What sense of continuity do these passages give you as a child of God?

The Job Description

◆ What then is this work that is both God's work in the larger story and Jesus' work in the human story? It could be called "show and tell": the fact that God loves humanity and desires to be in relationship with us by giving life. Seeing this love in action in Jesus, a love so deep it meant dying for it (John 15:12-13), and hearing it offered to all, believers become beneficiaries of that love by believing.

But they must also pass it on: "Just as I have loved you, you also should love one another" (13:34). ● This showing and telling of God's love for humanity is an integral part of receiving the love (15:14). Through others seeing this love in action in community, they come to believe (13:35). This was the work Jesus did for God, the work that was God's work in the world, and is the work of followers forever, guided by the Spirit. Followers of Jesus, however, are not servants, but friends, appointed to work at bearing fruit, as Jesus bore fruit for God (15:15-16). ■

Show and Tell

Were we to summarize the doctrine of John's Gospel then, Jesus' task was to show and tell God's promise of life in the presence of the Eternal. An encounter with Jesus demanded a decision to believe or not believe that what Jesus did and said was God's work. Salvation came with believing, entering at that moment into life with God.

For John, eternal life was immediate life in the presence of the Eternal, never interrupted even

◆ Where have you seen the love of God at work (a) in your life (b) in the life of your family and friends? What actions of Jesus can you find recorded in John's Gospel that illustrate how he demonstrated God's love in the world? What attracts you more about Jesus—what he said or what he did? Why?

● Read John 13:1-20, 31-35. What do you think the word *love* means in John? Is it just a feeling or is it action? How does he define *clean*? What is the role of the servant and messenger? Is there a call to justice along with love and servanthood in John? If so, how would you state it in your own words? What, if anything, does this call say to you?

■ Review John 15:1-17. What does Jesus mean by *friend*? Do you also qualify as a friend of Jesus, and he of you? How do you know? What are the marks of that friendship? Why, do you think, does Jesus in John's Gospel not instruct his followers to love their enemies, as in the Synoptic Gospels?

by death. ▲ Believing opens us to an emotional connection, a relationship of love (13:1, 34-35; 14:15), peace (14:27; 16:33; 20:19), and joy (15:11; 16:21-22; 17:13). Sin is the refusal to believe that God was at work in Jesus.

Judgment happens in the moment of refusal, not in a distant future. The judgment is to remain in darkness. When John the Baptist proclaimed that Jesus took away the sin of the world (1:29), he meant that, because of Jesus, people no longer needed to stay in the darkness of ignorance, but could come into the Light. To reject this offer through Jesus is to not believe, that is, sin, and thus enter into darkness (9:41).

Embracing the Invitation

▼ This encounter with "God at work" in Jesus is not limited to a first-century encounter. In Jesus, the possibility for an intimate relationship with God was proclaimed and realized and the invitation offered to believe it. The offer continues because the community of believers, with the indwelling Spirit, becomes the ongoing location of God's work of revealing this love. Encounters continue into the future as new generations see God's love at work and know that darkness is not the only choice now that God has chosen to dwell in the realm of human pain and darkness, bringing life and light.

◆ The promise of eternal life in John's Gospel is not that believers be removed from the world (17:15), but that a relationship with the eternal God and with each other around God's task begins and grows in the world (17:20-23). This oneness was good news for the Johannine community and still is for us.

▲ Read these Scriptures referring to love, peace, and joy. Life with the Eternal brings forth joy and peace. What do you think John means by joy and peace? Can peace be possible in a situation of persecution? If so, what sort of peace is it?

▼ If you were a persecuted member of the Johannine community, what would be the message of good news you would take away from this session? Is there a similar situation in your life to which this message can be applied?

◆ Jesus calls you to be a friend and messenger, to do God's work in the world. If you take this call seriously, in what way will (or does) it transform your life? Take time if you wish, to make or renew your commitment to carry on God's work in the world through the nudgings of the Spirit of love, joy, and peace.

JOHN'S MESSAGE

5

JOHN CLARIFIES OUR VISION

Two things had happened in the history of the Johannine community. Jesus had not returned to take them somewhere else or to set up a kingdom on earth, and they had been thrown out of Judaism, the only location for God they knew. John's Gospel was written to answer their question, "Where do we find God now?" The good news, John tells them, is that the Spirit (*Logos*) is already in their midst. They are the location of God in the world now!

God "Tenting" in the World

God has a history of abiding in the midst of the people. In the desert wanderings, God was not restricted anywhere, appearing in burning bushes, moving clouds, and as a voice in the strangest of situations. ● In order to localize God in some way for worship, the wandering Israelites built an ark (Exodus 25:10-16), placing it in a tabernacle when they paused from journeying (Exodus 26:1, 33-35). The ark of the covenant was not an image or idol. Such a replacement for God would have been unheard of (Exodus 20:1-5). The ark was the manifestation of God's presence and virtually identified with God, their covenant partner (Exodus 40:34-38). The ark as "God present" dwelled among them, God "tabernacling" or "pitching a tent" in their midst (John 1:14). The people approached God through the ark (Exodus 25:21-22).

When the first Temple was built in Jerusalem as the center of Israelite life (tenth century B.C.), this replaced the Tabernacle as the location for the ark, God's presence. When the Temple was destroyed at different times, its location on Mount Zion contin-

● Use a Bible dictionary to look up *ark of the covenant*, *Tabernacle*, and *Temple*. What do you know of Tabernacle and Temple rituals in Hebrew times? Read Exodus 25–26.

ued to signify God's presence with the people.

A second Temple was built in the sixth century B.C. after the Exile, and a third in Herod the Great's time (the Herod of Jesus' story). This Temple was destroyed in the Jewish war of A.D. 70. ■ With the Temple gone, synagogues had taken over as centers of Jewish life around the Torah— places where prayer, reading of Scripture, and teaching took place. It was from these synagogues that our Johannine community had been expelled.

John tells these readers, excluded from where God's presence had traditionally been located, that God has moved house and has "pitched a tent" for the divine presence (*Logos*) in the midst of the people, in the man Jesus. Jewish rabbinical theology of John's time talked of God's activity in the world as the *Shekinah*, from the verb "to tent" (Deuteronomy 12:2-7). John says that Jesus has become the new location for the *Shekinah* of God. Whether we use the term Logos,

Spirit, Sophia (Wisdom), Son of God, or *Shekinah*, it still means "God at work" in our midst, whether in a tent, temple, the Torah, or now, in Jesus. This is why John is careful to tell his two stories in parallel. Both an eternal history of God dwelling in the world and a human story of "God at work" in Jesus are present in John.

Located in Jesus

▲ According to John, by replacing Jewish buildings and institutions as the place of God's activity in the world, Jesus became the way (access) to God and the truth about God (14:6), the temple of God (2:18-22), the new place of worship (4:21), the new King of Israel (1:49). As the Son of God, Jesus followed in the line of Old Testament sons of God as God's emissaries (1:49; 2 Samuel 7:14; Psalms 2:7; 89:26). In Jesus, God reinterpreted sabbath (John 5:1-15) and Passover (6:1-15). Jesus became the living water and light of the world, replacing the Temple

■ Now look up *synagogue*. What is the significance of the synagogue to the Jewish people? Do you think of your church as the place for teaching? for prayer? for receiving the law of faithful living? Do you see the church as a place (or the place) where God lives? Explain.

▲ Divide these passages about God's activity in the world among the group members. Read each of the Scripture references. What does each say about Jesus? about how God is "located" in the world? About Jesus as "God with us"? about the way God works in each person?

rituals of water and light (7:37-39; 8:12-20). He was the good shepherd and gateway to the fold, in contrast to the false shepherds, the Pharisees (10:1-18); the new Lawgiver (13:34); and the access to the offer of eternal life (11:25-27).

None of these images would have been lost on the hearers. If Jesus was the new center for "God with us," not the synagogue, and they were followers of Jesus with the Spirit in their midst, then they were now the location of God's presence in the world, God's new house. They were already living life in the company of the Eternal.

In Hebrew history, the continuity of God's activity in the world was not the place where God was present but the fact that God was present in a relationship with them. God's desire has been the same from the beginning. Thus, when John talks of God's activity in the world, he is talking about God's continuing desire to be in relationship—to love humanity. This is the story of the *Logos*, the story of heavenly things that Nicodemus could not see (17:15-19).

Heavenly Things

▼ In Hebrew Scriptures, *heavenly* had two meanings. It referred to the firmament, that physical dome of sky that covered the earth. *Heavenly* also referred to God's presence and activity (1 Kings 8:27-30) that was never restricted to the distant blue dome, but could be anywhere in the created world and beyond. As Solomon said at the dedication of the first Temple: "But will God indeed dwell on the earth? Even heaven and the highest heaven cannot contain you, much less this house that I have built!" (1 Kings 8:27).

When the second Temple was built, the people were warned that the Creator of the world could not be contained in a house built by human hands. What kept God present with the people depended, not on a temple, but on a right attitude among the worshipers (Isaiah 66:1-2). References, therefore, to God's house in the Old Testament were to God's household, the covenantal relationship shared with those with whom God lived. There might also have been a location, such as the Temple. But for a traveling God, the members of God's household were those who trav-

---

▼ Review this text about the meanings of the term *heavenly*. Look up the beginning of the Creation story in Genesis 1 and the comment in 1 Kings 8:27-30 to see how the firmament is described and how God's dwelling place is described. How would you describe God's "house"?

eled with God rather than the places in which they stayed.

◆ John has this idea when he talks of the Father's house and of abiding in the Father. This place is not located far away (a place called heaven), but is here and now in a heavenly sphere, *heavenly* meaning where God is present and at work. It is the household of those who live with God. The offer of eternal life with God (the work of God Jesus was sent to do) is effective immediately in the heavenly presence of God with other believers, a relationship of love beginning in the world. It is different from the relationships and way of life of the world (life in the light, not in darkness). This participation in God's household, while still part of the human story is, at the same time, participation in the larger story. ● The eternal life and career of the *Logos* is present in the world, but is not restricted to any location, even the flesh of Jesus (John 3:12).

The Incarnation of God

■ Because of this idea that in Jesus, God has "pitched a tent" among the people, the whole Incarnation—"God at work" in the total life of the man Jesus becomes the central activity of God in John's Gospel. It is more than simply the events around Jesus' death and resurrection, the emphasis of the other Gospels. Communicating God's offer of love through the works and words of Jesus filled the whole span of this man's working life, beginning with Jesus' baptism and ending with his death. The death of Jesus therefore, was a moment of glory because God's revealing work was done—"It is finished!" (19:30).

But only John's first story ends there—the human story of Jesus— not the larger story of God's ongoing activity in the world that was from the beginning (14:15-20). ▲ The appearances to the disciples after Jesus' death are part

◆ What do you think John means when he talks of earthly and heavenly things (John 3:12)? Would you use those terms today? Are there better ones for the distinction John makes? If so, what are they?

● How do you think modern science and technology affect our images of heaven and earth? Can we talk of where God is in the same way? Where is God for you?

■ What does it mean to say John concentrates on the Incarnation while other Gospels concentrate on Jesus' death and resurrection? What is the significance of Jesus' death for John?

of this larger story. What the disciples discover through these appearances is that, although the Jesus they knew and loved as a friend and teacher had died and was no longer with them as a human being, the relationship with God that they had seen lived out in the life of Jesus, and into which they had already entered through Jesus' invitation—the eternal household of God (17:22-23)—had not been destroyed by Jesus' death. They were still experiencing it! The heavenly relationship with the Father and with Jesus in Jesus' lifetime had survived physical death. In the same way, this relationship would also survive their physical deaths. This was the greatest sign of all! This was the good news!

▼ Furthermore, what the disciples discovered was that they were the new location of this heavenly community with God. They were the household of God where God was at work in the world. They were now the earthly location of the larger story, a new incarnation, as it were.

Another human episode began as the disciples received the Holy Spirit (20:22), just as Jesus had received the Spirit at his baptism (1:32). The career of the *Logos* in the world—inviting humanity into the household of God, the larger story—would continue in them and will continue in every new community of believers who offers this eternal life, first made accessible through the work of Jesus (17:6-21). The Johannine community would know this referred to them. We twenty-first–century readers know this also is us.

Life in the Presence of the Eternal

As I have said earlier, when we read the different Gospels as originally written (different community stories developing different grand metaphors and images of "God at work" in humanity), rather than cutting and pasting the stories together as if the themes are all the same, we discover all sorts of new things we had previously not seen. John does not create something new by talking of eternal life and

▲ How do you understand John 14 in light of this study? Is this passage only for funerals? How does it help us look at our own death differently?

▼ Read these passages about the reception of the Holy Spirit. Why, do you think, did the disciples receive the Spirit at the post-death appearances in John, rather than at Pentecost (Acts 2)?

heaven as present realities. Rather he affirms the existing Hebrew idea of God present in the world, the unrestricted divine Spirit that blows where it chooses like the wind. We hear but do not know where it comes from or goes (3:8). ◆ To live with a God who is everywhere and anywhere and always is not about a place—where would that be?—but about a relationship with God, wherever God is, now and forever. It has nothing to do with physical death, because the power of death to separate us from this life with God has been reduced to nothing with God's offer to dwell with us and us with God. According to John, one remains in the full presence of God during life and after death (11:25-26).

Though death is a defining moment for our experience as humans, it is not the defining moment where God is concerned. For John, eternal life, life with God, begins when we choose not to continue in darkness—the human condition. It does not start at death or at some end-time judgment. Eternal life begins in the moment we encounter "God at work" somewhere in the world—the larger story—and make the choice between entering into life with God or turning from the Light toward a life without God. The choice is not about heaven or hell, but about accepting or rejecting a relationship, the indwelling presence of God. For John, eternal life is about living, not dying.

● John has prepared for us a veritable art gallery of masterpieces on the theme of living now and always in the presence of God. The first canvas is of living in the presence of the Light where everything is clearly seen, rather than in darkness. The next painting is of healthy branches flourishing on a nourishing vine, living fruitfully and abundantly under the care of a master vinedresser, God. The next is the image of a hillside at dusk as a faithful shepherd herds sheep into a secure sheepfold, locks the door, and stands guard all night so the sheep can sleep in peace. The

◆ What do you make of the idea that living with God has nothing to do with physical death and that the power of death has been reduced to nothing? Read John 11:25-26. What does this tell you about your own eternity?

● What is your favorite masterpiece in John's art gallery of portraits about living in the presence of God? Why? How does it help you understand who God is and what your relationship with God is?

JOHN'S MESSAGE

next painting is of a loving household of sons and daughters, brothers and sisters, servants who become friends, all gathered together and thriving under loving and caring parental eyes.

According to John, eternal life, the whole point of John's Gospel, is about how we live our lives now, not about how we end them.

The Right Credentials

What can we learn from John about living in this eternal household of God today? ■ First, it is very clear that, for John, there are insiders and outsiders, and this depends on whether you believe in Jesus. "Yes!" some might be thinking, mentally listing those we think are outsiders, according to our particular criteria. Others of us, the inveterate doubters who sit in church pews and ask all the questions that are not even to be thought about, might be a little disappointed, assuming once again that we must be outsiders.

However, we will be surprised if we look a little closer.

▲ All the wrong sorts of people seemed to believe for all the wrong reasons when they encountered Jesus. The Samaritan woman was an outsider on two counts in this Jewish story (4:1-42). The blind man did not even know who Jesus was when he believed in him and did not seem phased at his ignorance when the Pharisees questioned him (9:1-41). The disabled man had little faith that Jesus could do anything anyway and had pretty much given up on everything (5:1-18). The royal officer believed, without any proof, that Jesus had healed his son, even though the distance between Cana and Capernaum separated healer and patient (4:46-54).

▼ Those who should have immediately seen the connections and signed up with Jesus hesitated and seemed confused or blinded, such as Nicodemus, a teacher of Jewish Law (3:1-10).

■ List as many of the insiders and outsiders of John's community as you can. Are those same persons or groups of persons still considered in or out? Why?

▲ Review these stories again briefly to see how these outsiders related to Jesus and he to them. Do you see yourself in some of these stories? If so, how, and as whom?

▼ Next review the stories about those who were, or should have been on the "inside." How would you compare and contrast the insiders with the outsiders? What ironies do you see? what moral lessons? what faith lessons?

Peter's boisterous enthusiasm and protestations of faithfulness simply dissolved under opposition (18:15-27). The other disciples just did not get it, no matter how often Jesus spelled it out (16:29-33). Simple folk watched the greatest of signs and were still suspicious (7:10-13). Judas left a supper table surrounded by such intensity of love only to turn his teacher over to the authorities (13:21-30).

If one were to draw up a cultural profile of those most likely to believe from the stories John selects to tell us about encounters with Jesus, we would be lost! The profile would not necessarily include those with the most sin or those who knew their theology best. Jesus makes this very clear in the story of the blind man. Neither would it be those who spent the most time with Jesus and had experienced God's love. Judas betrayed him, Peter denied him, and the others seemed very dense about the whole experience.

But that is the whole point. That is why John selected the stories he did (20:31). It is all in the encounter with "God at work" in the world, whether through Jesus for those who lived during Jesus' lifetime, through the Spirit's prompting in the Johannine community in John's day, or through encounters with the thousands of communities and individuals now and throughout the twenty-first century who continue to believe that God is at work in the world and who live in ways that show this to be true for them.

◆ *Believing,* for John, was about seeing a sign and believing the sign read "God at work," whatever that sign may be. This challenges us not to try to define how God can work in the world—to confine "God at work" to our categories, doctrines, and expectations. What John shows us by the stories he selects is that "God at work" continually surprises us, breaking out of our boxes as fast as we can build them.

The blind man's neighbors did not believe because they had always known the man as blind and could not think of him differently. The Pharisees would not believe because of their central litmus test that God would not work through someone who did not follow their Jewish rules. When they could not verify Jesus' background or training, they attacked the blind man for his misplaced faith in a nonaccredited teacher (9:28-29). They were

---

◆ What does *believe* mean? Whom would your definition include or exclude? What about those who do not know what they believe? Is John talking about a believing church or individuals? What difference does it make to believe we are living eternal life now?

JOHN'S MESSAGE

looking for a Jewish Messiah who would perfectly fulfill Jewish law, but God's larger story was not confined by religious pedigrees. The parents shrank from committing themselves at all. We will never know what they really thought because they were too afraid to take a stand (9:20-23). In contrast, the blind man continued unperturbed. All he knew was that, because of this encounter with God in Jesus, he could finally see and had entered into a world of Light, not darkness.

The Household of God

● Perhaps the biggest challenge for us today from John's insider-outsider categories is that these are not determined by belief in a creed, a doctrinal statement, or an institution's credentials. In fact, John gives very little support for the doctrinal wars Christians have battled for centuries. The people who believed came from diverse backgrounds that crossed social classes—the wealthy Joseph of Arimathea (19:38); fishermen (21:3); Martha, a female head of a household (11:1-44); a blind man (9:1-41); and a lame beggar (5:1-15). They also represented different religious beliefs—Nicodemus, a member of the Sanhedrin, although we never know what he finally decides, except that he brought spices for Jesus' burial (3:1-21; 7:45-52; 19:38-42); the Samaritan woman who persuaded her whole community to believe (4:5-42); and some Greeks who came to see Jesus (12:20-26).

There seemed to be no catechism to learn, no confession of sin to be made, no doctrinal statement to sign, not even a correct ritual to follow. Everyone who believed that in Jesus they witnessed "God at work" was welcome in the household of God, a household without hierarchy where all shared equally in the work—to love one another and to bear fruit by this love attracting others (13:34-35; 15:15-17).

Scholars have debated about what John says about *church*. Quite obviously for John, churches are households of God who love one another. However, *church* has historically been defined as the place where the sacraments are celebrated and the word of God is preached, tasks

---

● John includes all believers in the household of God, though they cross social and cultural classes. Quickly review these passages that give a brief portrait of a cross section of believers. Does anything unify them or identify them together? If so, what? How would you describe the "qualifications" for membership in the household of God? What is it that makes you a member?

done by a special, ordained ministry. Yet John has no institution of a Eucharist as a sacramental remembrance ritual, a central event for today's church with ecumenical arguments focusing not just on how it should be done, but who can do it, and who can sit together at the table.

Eucharistic Imagery

■ The event in John that comes closest to a hint of a Eucharist is the feeding of the five thousand (John calls it a large crowd) and the discourse that followed about the bread of life (6:1-59). Prior to this event, Jesus had spoken about drinking living water and now speaks of bread being eaten. The event takes place near Passover, but in a field in Galilee, not an upper room in Jerusalem. If this event rang bells for the Johannine community as an equivalent of a Eucharistic meal, it is interesting that, in John's account, the distribution of the loaves and fishes is done by Jesus, whereas in the other Gospels, it is the disciples who distribute the food. Whether John intended this as a type of Eucharist, albeit an alternative one more inclusive as to who receives food and who serves it, we cannot say. What we do know is that another intriguing thing happened at John's last supper in terms of community ritual.

A "Share" in the "Work of God"

▲ John's account of Jesus' public ministry and signs ends in Chapter 12. Chapter 13 changes direction as Jesus concentrates on the insiders, instructing them about their future in the world after his death. These instructions are given at supper the night before Jesus' death, a supper not limited to the Twelve.

During the meal, Jesus arose from the table, wrapped a towel

■ Read John 6:1-59. Compare this story with the passages describing a Eucharistic meal in the other Gospels (Matthew 26:26-29; Mark 14:22-25; Luke 22:15-20). What are the similarities and differences? What images does Jesus use to explain this event? What does the story of feeding the crowd tell you about Jesus?

▲ What do you think John's story of the footwashing means? Read John 13:1-20. What happens? What does this story tell you about leadership? about servanthood? about hospitality? about "sharing" with Jesus? Have you ever participated in a footwashing service? What was that experience like? Should footwashing be a regular part of our worship practices today? Why or why not?

about his waist and washed the feet of his guests, an act recorded only in John (13:1-20). Not only does Jesus wash their feet, he also tells them, despite Peter's protests, that this is what they must continue doing for each other (13:14-15). Now footwashing was a customary act of hospitality when someone entered a house, usually done by a servant, or sometimes pupils did it for their teacher. Because this action preserved certain conventions of hierarchy, Peter protested the reversal of roles—Jesus his teacher acting as pupil or servant. Jesus tells Peter that, unless he accepts this in this household (God's) where no one, not even teachers, are greater than another, he cannot "share" with Jesus (13:8).

This "sharing" was more than simple fellowship. It was the word in Hebrew history for a tribal share in the Promised Land, a heritage from God to all but the tribe of Levi (Numbers 18:20; Deuteronomy 12:12; 14:27). In Revelation's apocalyptic vision, this share is described as a heavenly reward (Revelation 20:6).

Jesus is therefore telling Peter that, in the household of God to which they already belong, entry depends on and is symbolized by this ritual of footwashing. They are commanded to do it for one another as a sign, not just of mutual residence in God's household, but as a recognition that all hierarchies—servant and master, pupil and teacher (and we can add clergy and lay)—are broken down.

▼ We miss the point if we use this symbol today to talk about servant leadership by those who are ordained in order to hush critics who point to our separation of God's household into two—ordained and lay. Nowhere in John do we find any hint of a separate ministry or elevated professional role in the community of believers. John's metaphors for community point away from this.

The metaphor of the vine and branches gives no support to different types of branches with different functions—all branches serve the same purpose on one central vine, Jesus. The metaphor of the good shepherd mentions no hierarchy among sheep, and the shepherd refers to Jesus. There is no commissioning of Twelve to take over this pastoral role as special representatives of Jesus, or to carry on his ministry in some exclusive way. In fact, the Twelve

▼ Why do we ordain people? What is the distinction between clergy and lay? What happens at ordination? Which are ordained tasks and which lay tasks? Where do we find support for this difference in John? in other Scripture?

are scarcely mentioned in John. ◆ Jesus' words to his followers were always a general invitation to all believers to share the work of God in God's household.

A Discipleship of Equals in the Household of God?

Even the metaphor of Father and Son does not allow a hierarchy in the household of God. All are friends of God, not children and servants (15:15-17). All are siblings with Jesus of the one Father (20:17). Some have argued a special representative role of shepherd for Peter from Jesus' words in John about feeding his sheep (21:15-19). But if we look closer, we find those words were more about restoring Peter to the fold after his triple denial of Jesus than an honor of any kind that puts him over the rest of the sheep. This is especially true in the whole context of John's Gospel where Peter's actions are less than favorable in comparison with the unnamed beloved disciple (18:10-11, 15-27; 19:25-27; 20:1-10; 21:1-23).

● We might ask: What was John suggesting to his readers by including the footwashing? What does this say to us today? Why has this act, carrying with it a command for repetition as a symbolic act of inclusion and equality in the household of God, been for the most part ignored by the church? Why has the Eucharistic meal, not mentioned in John, become not only central to the church, but overlaid with rules of hierarchy and exclusion as to who can dispense it and who can receive it—rules not mentioned in the original final supper? Today's Christians, embroiled in crippling debates about which is the true household of God and who is included and excluded, need to ask such questions of even its most ancient traditions of sacraments and ordination. ■ Is John showing us an alternative vision of what it is to be the church, the household of God, a discipleship of equals?

◆ What is a call to ministry? Who receives such calls? How does this fit with John's community doing God's work in the world? What can we learn from John about living in community as a discipleship of equals?

● How would you describe the church from John's Gospel? What would you describe as the true household of God?

■ Jesus continues to love and welcome all believers into God's household (see John 16:27; 17:20-21). Take time in prayer to hear these words of welcome to *you* and believe them.

6

JOHN LOOKS AT THE NEW MILLENNIUM

Even though millennia are merely figures and numbers on a calendar, they do focus our attention in a special way. ▲ Like New Year's resolutions, they encourage us to look ahead to the next one thousand years, asking questions about who we are, where are we going, and what changes we need to make to move in new directions. It is appropriate to ask such questions of John, poised as he and his community were, at the brink of a new century.

A Look at Outsiders

▼ The last chapter focused on John's message to insiders. In this chapter I want to ask some twenty-first–century questions of John about outsiders in a pluralis-tic world. This is not to say John's world was not pluralistic. John's world had many cultures and religions sharing the same space. Because of this, John should have something to say to us about being a Christian community in such a society.

However, we are also inheritors of not only John's first-century advice to a minority group against a hostile majority but also of John's advice interpreted later by a dominant religion to justify actions in history that wreaked havoc on other minority religions and cultures. John's assurance to a powerless few that they were the true children of God sounds different in the hands of a majority with power to use such a truth claim as a weapon for the oppres-

▲ What sort of New Year's resolutions do you make? Do you have some for the new millennium?

▼ What does it mean for us to talk about a pluralistic world? How would you define "insiders" and "outsiders" in your culture? in your church? Do you identify with being either an insider or an outsider? How does that feel?

sion and destruction of others who do not "have the truth." ◆

This oppression happened in Christian history with the colonization of indigenous people across the world and in the Jewish Holocaust, to name just two events. As twenty-first–century Christians, we must acknowledge this part of our history as well, especially when statements such as these in John's Gospel have been used to justify such action.

The Question of the Jews

● As we have seen throughout this study, John had strong words to say about "the Jews," not against Judaism as such. He portrays Jesus as a Jew within Jewish history and a new location of God's activity. Many Jews believed in Jesus. Others remained undecided (7:15, 25-27, 45-48; 10:21), questioned his credentials (2:18; 3:1-2, 9; 5:10-12; 6:41-42; 9:16), turned away

(8:43-45, 59; 10:20), or opposed him to the point of killing him (5:16-8; 7:1; 10:31, 39; 11:46-53). Sometimes John clarifies which Jews he is talking about, such as the Pharisees or the Sanhedrin, but often says simply "the Jews." This does not happen in the same way in the other Gospels where the audiences were still, if precariously, part of a synagogue and still Jews. The Jewish authorities were the opposition.

John's statements about "the Jews" reflect the different situation of his community. "The Jews" were those who had remained in the synagogue, unbelievers, as opposed to those who believed in Jesus and had been expelled. Jewishness was not the issue, since many of the Johannine community had Jewish heritage.

■ The issue was belief in or rejection of Jesus. However, when such hostile statements are hurled at these unbelievers under the

---

◆ Inside/outside thinking and behavior occurs when a dominant group claims a privilege and exercises its collective power to determine what is proper. What do you know about the shift from minority to majority status for Christians and for the church? What do you think about the Holocaust as a Christian? Did "the Jews" kill Jesus? What does this mean for today?

● Review at least several of these passages concerning "the Jews." How does John portray Jesus' understanding of and relationship with "the Jews"? Does this term refer to every Jewish person? certain persons?

■ The unbelievers or Jews are portrayed as a hostile group responsible for Jesus' crucifixion. Look up these passages for the portrait they paint. What is the cumulative effect?

label of "the Jews" (1:10-11; 3:18-20; 5:39-49; 8:39-49; 16:2-3), especially when it is "the Jews" in John who bear responsibility for Jesus' arrest and crucifixion (7:1, 32-36, 44; 11:45-57; 18:1-14, 28-40; 19:6-7, 12-16), John's Gospel leaves itself open to future generations of Christians to turn the words into justification for the persecution and exclusion of the Jewish people on a grand scale throughout history.

How to Read the Story

▲ Having just come through a century when some of the most horrific crimes were committed against Jews, we must ask what to do with these texts in John, especially when they occur in a Gospel that describes the Christian community almost exclusively by love. Do we leave such verses out of our lectionaries or alter the translations so they sound less accusatory? Such actions may make those who recognize the problem more aware, but do nothing about those who read the words without thought for their original context and persist in persecuting Jews today, either as the "killers of Jesus" or as "unbelievers."

The other side of the anti-Jewish coin is less obvious but still hinders understanding between Jews and Christians today. Because John's Gospel argues that Jesus was the replacement of Jewish institutions and rituals, the Hebrew Scriptures and Judaism have been regarded by Christians as the prologue to the Christian story, as indicated by our use of the terms *Old Testament* and *New Testament*. Even though they were separated from the synagogue, John's audience understood the replacement themes within Jewish history. Future generations, however, raised as Christians in a climate not only devoid of a knowledge of Judaism but also geared to its rejection as a superseded religion, have made the story of Jesus a Christian story, with Jesus the first Christian. This identification has created a Christianity ignorant of Jesus' real context, making it difficult to appreciate the full significance of what Jesus said and did.

Jesus in His Jewish Context

When Jesus stands in the Temple on the last day of the festival and proclaims he is the living water (7:37-38) and the light of the

---

▲ What do you think should be done with these texts in John? How do we deal responsibly with the biblical texts when they seem to contradict other messages of the Bible, such as the inclusive and loving nature of God?

world (8:12), it makes a difference to know that this Festival of Tabernacles was an eight-day festival of both light and water.▼ During the celebrations, huge candles set on lampstands lit the whole Jerusalem sky, symbolizing the light of God. A water ceremony was enacted in which the priests brought water from the pool of Siloam and poured it on the Temple altar as a libation— "living" water (running water) as opposed to stagnant water.

Zechariah 14 was read at the festival, a passage that talks of an expected messiah whose appearance would bring continuous light, and living water would flow out from Jerusalem (Zechariah 14:6-8). This messiah would be king over all the earth (14:9).

With such knowledge behind us, the impact of Jesus' actions blows us away. He had interrupted the feast to announce he was their expected light and water. No wonder the crowd debated furiously whether he was the Messiah. No wonder some wanted to arrest him then and there (John 7:40-44).

◆ In order to be more faithful Christians, one of our twenty-first–century resolutions should be to renew the conversation with Judaism, the religion of Jesus, so we can learn from each other as we share common roots. Some of the most wonderful stories that make newspaper headlines today are those when brothers and sisters, separated at birth, find each other many years later and realize how many common traits, noble dreams, and intense feelings they share from a common heritage. May this be the experience of Jews and Christians in the twenty-first century!

Absolute Truth Claims

The Jews have not been the only ones in history to experience the effect of the insider-outsider language of John's Gospel. On the strength of the verse "Jesus said to him, 'I am the way, and the truth, and the life. No one comes to the Father except through me'" (14:6), Christians through the centuries have made exclusive claims on God that have resulted, on a

▼ When John presents Jesus as the replacement of Jewish institutions and rituals, what did that mean to Jesus' hearers? to us today? Read Zechariah 14. What are the stated expectations of the Messiah?

◆ Do you think of Jesus as a Jew or as a Christian? Have you discussed Jesus with any Jewish people? How does a greater awareness of Jesus' own traditions of ritual and worship enhance your understanding of him as the Messiah?

global scale, in religions and cultures being wiped out under Christian colonization. Those non-Christian countries that had the strength to resist found themselves locked in wars fought in the name of the God of love. Even within Christianity, such claims for the possession of absolute truth still pit individuals and denominations against one another.

Some Christians may still want to read these words from John in exclusive terms, but others find this more difficult now. Can we really claim John's Gospel is about loving one another, yet look at our next door neighbor, our doctor, our children's school teacher, who might be Muslim or Buddhist or Catholic or Unitarian, and say, depending on our particular criteria for truth, that there is no truth in their traditions?

● This verse, as any verse, needs to be read in its context in order to see what it means now. The disciples have been told Jesus is about to leave them, to die. Jesus explains that, since his death completes his task of offering a life with God, it will have created (prepared) for them the right of residence in his "Father's house." This spiritual household of God, for John, is here and now and always, in the heavenly presence of God (14:2-3).

Jesus says he will come again and take them "to himself," "include them with him" in this life in God's presence (household) from now on. This is exactly what the disciples experienced in the post-Easter appearances. The relationship they had experienced with Jesus and the Father had not been destroyed with Jesus' death, but continued intact! Jesus assures them, "You know the place where I am going." He has been telling them about this life with God not defined by space or time since the beginning of his ministry.

Jesus as Their Access to God

Once again, as always, the disciples misunderstand, thinking Jesus is off some place without telling them where. How then can they find the way to him?—a very human question. Jesus reminds them he has always been, for them, both the access (way) to this life with God and also the true demonstrable example of what this life with God looks like: the way, the truth and the life (14:6). This claim of Jesus was not intended as an isolated statement to be used alone as the exclusive

● What do you think John 14:6 meant to the disciples? What does it mean for the Christian community? for other faith groups? What claims for Christianity would you make from it?

claim of Christianity over all religions throughout global history.

At this point, Jesus was hardly even making the claim for Christianity, but as God's new location in Judaism, which many Jews had rejected. It was simply an assurance of good news for a group of Jewish people who had lost their previous access or way to God through the synagogue. They would have been familiar with what John meant by the "way." It was a life lived in accordance with Jewish law (Psalms 119:1, 3, 5; 86:11).

Once again, John was simply continuing his original theme. Access to God is through Jesus who had replaced the Jewish Tabernacle, Temple, rituals, and now the way of the Law, as the place of "God at work" in their world. "No one comes to the Father but by me" can better be said in context, "None of *you* come to the Father but by me."

What we have seen all along in John are the two stories. The story of Jesus is the Jewish story of "God at work" in their history. The larger story is the career of the *Logos* in the world, beginning at its creation and continuing into the future as guiding Spirit. While Jesus was the way for his followers to gain access to God in their time, what about the career of the *Logos* from the beginning in other parts of the *Logos's* universe?

■ The ancient Near East was not the totality of the world. What was the creating and revealing God doing, for example, in Africa at the same time? Was the working and traveling God busy there as well? What of other cultures with whom we now come in contact in our expanded world who also claim to have a particular story of "God at work" that shapes their lives? Can they have truth as well?

Many Christians will not be comfortable with this line of talk if they read John 14:6 beyond the Johannine situation. But in the global village of the twenty-first century, such questions need to be, and will be, asked. Within the Johannine context of outsiders, whose access to the way through Judaism had been blocked, this assurance of John 14:6 can be appreciated. Jesus offered them a new way to God. Does this, however, bind the "God at work" of our larger story to revealing activity in only one cultural and historical context of the world? If God is the creating and revealing One from the beginning, is it not rea-

■ Missionary endeavor to spread Christianity often replaced, rather than incorporated, indigenous cultures and religions. Do you think it was a good or bad thing? a necessary change? Why?

sonable to ask if this Creator God was *also* the revealing One in Australia or the Americas before missionaries brought the story of Jesus to them?

Aboriginal Christians Reclaim Their Stories

▲ Australian Aboriginal Christian leaders have asked these questions. While recognizing Christian zeal in sharing the Gospel, they regret that it was at the expense of their own culture. They liken western colonization to the ficus, a parasitic fig plant that germinates high in the branches of the Kauri pine in the rainforest, sending down snake-like roots to the soil. In time, these roots thicken, strangling the host tree, and the fig lives on in its stead.

In the same way, the Christian message was often imposed from without, choking indigenous spiritual traditions, rather than being planted in the new soil to grow into a shape within that cultural environment. This is not just talk. Aboriginal people believe their land was entrusted to them by the Creator Spirit; and, without their ceremonies and culture, they cannot properly care for the land.

Thus, they feel lost and shamed.

Aboriginal Christian leaders find John's Gospel helpful with its two stories. For them, the Jewish story of "God at work" in the world is not the only story of "God at work" from the beginning. They too have a story about "God at work" from the beginning of Aboriginal culture—how the world came into being and how they experienced the Creator Spirit, known by many names.

Their creation story is similar to the Jewish story in many ways—a void changed by dynamic, creating activity bringing life. Yet, although the missionaries claimed God was everywhere and existed from the beginning of Creation, this was rarely interpreted to suggest that God was present in the stories of Aboriginal people from the beginning.

Peoples of the Land

Aboriginal Christians talk about the Creator Spirit assigning them to specific relationships with the land—not so different from "God at work" in the Hebrew people. Aboriginal ceremonies celebrate their relationship with the land and the law, just as the Israelites

▲ What do you think of claims by Aboriginal Christians that God was at work in their culture from the beginning? (Native American and many Hispanic cultures, for example, also weave the Christian and indigenous faith beliefs together.) What, do you think, is the effect on Christianity? Is it strengthened or weakened? Explain.

celebrated relationship to God through land and covenantal law.

The Creator Spirit for Aborigines is life-giving power, just as *Logos*, God's creative activity, was the giver of life from the beginning (1:1-5). While *Logos* is not in the Aboriginal vocabulary, Aboriginal Christians can identify with an image of a mysterious power of God, the ordering principle of the world, "pitching a tent" among them (1:14).

Like Hebrew people, they have nomadic roots and know about a Creator Spirit traveling with them, "pitching a tent" or "camping" with them and being present in their ceremonies and sacred sites. ▼ The story of Jesus as part of the larger story of the Creator Spirit "God at work" in the whole world resonates with their experience, as it did for the Johannine community. The Creator Spirit desired to be in relationship with humanity from the beginning and has now "pitched a tent" among us in the flesh and continues to "camp" with us as the Spirit in the world.

A Defining Human Story

Many more examples of Christians around the world recognizing there are two stories at play in their lives at any time abound. They look at their own particular stories as signs of the larger story of "God at work" in the world. The first-century Jewish story is Christianity's defining story of God's encounter with humanity. But the story of "God at work" relating with humanity, the larger story, is repeated in every human community of the Spirit throughout the world and through history.

This story will continue to be repeated in the expanses of everything we know as the universe and beyond, now and in the future. Just as John's community heard the story of Jesus reinterpreted for their situation as good news in crisis, so we continue to reinterpret the story of Jesus as good news for our story and context, whatever that might be.

Women Retell Their Stories

Women have reinterpreted John's story of Jesus so it becomes good news for their experience. John shows that Jesus counted women among his most faithful and productive disciples, and his encounters with them revealed profound truths about God's offer of love. The first sign was organized by Jesus' mother (2:1-11). The Samaritan woman understood Jesus' message and was the first person to bring a whole (foreign) community to belief (4:1-42).◆

▼ Do you think God is at work in religions other than Christianity? In what way?

Friends Martha and Mary played key roles in the raising of Lazarus, and Martha's comments revealed Jesus as the resurrection and the life (11:1-44). Mary also was the first to foreshadow Jesus' impending death by anointing his feet for burial (12:1-8).

Women, together with the beloved disciple, were the only ones mentioned as remaining with Jesus as he died (19:25-27). Mary Magdalene discovered the empty tomb first, encountered the glorified Jesus first, and was the first to tell all the disciples the good news (20:1-18).

● Such "looking again" at the stories in John's Gospel reveals the Samaritan woman, like the blind man, as a model disciple (4:1-42). Although her character has been painted in history as doubtful, John does not suggest this. Her numerous marriages most likely reflected the necessity for widows in that society to marry again, often the brothers of their dead husbands.

Her amazement at Jesus' knowledge of her situation does not indicate shame but, as with Nathanael (1:45-51), proof that Jesus was truly sent from God. Once we free ourselves of unfounded assumptions about her morals, we see the real honor afforded her as a disciple, the first "apostle" beyond Judaism.

Unlike Nicodemus, who had every reason as a Jewish intellectual to recognize Jesus as the Messiah but hesitated to do so, the Samaritan woman not only listened to Jesus but raised the key theological argument separating Jews and Samaritans (4:19-24). She believed Jesus was the Messiah, and her village accepted her invitation to come and see, hardly the response to a woman of uncertain moral character (4:1-42).

Assurance for Outsiders

While many people today hear John's comforting words of "abiding in God" in the security of privileged First-World lifestyles, John was addressing a marginalized community hated by the world and persecuted, as Jesus

◆ Read these stories of women's involvement in Jesus' ministry. How did they contribute? How does the fact that Jesus counted women as close disciples help women today? What is women's place in the church?

● Review the story of the Samaritan woman in John 4:1-42. How have you understood this story? the character of the woman? Does the interpretation in this chapter add to or change your understanding of her and her effect on the faith community? Explain. What new insight to faith does it give you?

had been (15:18-25; 16:31-33).■ Not only were they excluded, they were also a collection of outcasts within themselves: Samaritans, the lame, the blind, the unschooled, women.

They heard Jesus telling them they would be thrown out of the synagogue, torn from their roots, and even killed by those who claim to do the will of God (16:2). The gradual buildup of hostile story after hostile story of Jesus' rejection, even to death, showed Jesus as marginalized and persecuted as they were, eventually paying the highest price for his refusal to abandon the work God gave him to do (12:27; 18:11). John's asides about people not declaring their beliefs publicly or denying Jesus (7:12-13; 9:22-23; 18:15-17, 25-27; 19:38) contrast with those who boldly professed their faith under attack (5:10-12; 9:26-34).

John describes living in a community of love that personifies the greatest love of all, divine love, and working in unity and harmony around a calling, God's work. This description literally shines before us in its brilliance, in contrast to the hostile, outside world. For twenty-first–century people living as refugees, displaced persons, orphans, abused women and children, convicted criminals, victims of injustice, or those who are just plain lonely and unloved, the promise of being bathed in God's love in a loving community of faith in the midst of an unjust and evil world, offers hope and life.

While some have used John to justify withdrawal from and superiority over the world while awaiting removal to higher places, marginalized and oppressed communities can hear John's message as assurance within this world, empowering them to move out again into the world to challenge all the powers that oppress and destroy. ▲ This is the good news. Come and see!

■ What are the strengths and weaknesses of John's insider-outsider talk? How have these studies helped you see your situation? How does Jesus' teaching and action model for us the loving attitude toward refugees, displaced persons, and other vulnerable persons?

▲ Pray for those whom society considers outsiders and then for those who consider themselves insiders. Jesus' criterion in John for insiders and outsiders was very clear. He asked Peter, "Do you love me?" Peter replied, "Yes, Lord, you know that I love you." Jesus said to him, "Follow me" (21:15-19) Now hear the question from Jesus for yourself, "Do you love me?" If you so desire, make your own personal response, in word and action.